OPERATIONS RESEARCH
IN IRELAND

Operations Research in Ireland

Edited by
Julian MacAirt
Senior Lecturer, Statistics,
Trinity College Dublin

THE MERCIER PRESS
CORK and DUBLIN

The Mercier Press Limited
4 Bridge Street, Cork *and*
24 Lower Abbey Street, Dublin 1

British Library Cataloguing in Publication Data
Operations research
   1. Management. Problem solving. Applications of
operations research
I. MacAirt, Julian
658.4'034

ISBN 0-85342-862-X

The editor and publishers gratefully acknowledge the generous sponsorship given by the following companies and institutions:
CARA Data Processing
Trinity Trust
Allied Irish Banks
System Dynamics
Craig Gardner
NIHE Limerick, Mathematics Department
Microdigital Business Services
(Shankill Office Centre)

Cover design by Joseph Gervin
Typeset in Bembo by Kononia Limited, Manchester
Printed by Leinster Leader Ltd., Naas

CONTENTS

To Nora and Ber

FOREWORD

It is a pleasure for me to contribute the foreword to this unique record of Operations Research practice in Ireland, the first general textbook on the subject. It contains numerous case studies which will be of great use in teaching the subject in universities. The successful applications of OR described in the book will also be of interest to academic and business practitioners in other small open economies throughout the world. Furthermore, the appendices give a detailed account, for the first time, of OR research and teaching in the Irish universities, both north and south.

This book celebrates the 21st anniversary of the founding of the Operations Research Society of Ireland. The Society took its place on the world stage in 1972, when it hosted the VIth World Conference on Operations Research on behalf of the International Federation of Operations Research Societies (IFORS).

Operations Research, as a profession and separate discipline, had its origins in Britain during World War II, when the threat of U-boat attack on shipping was at its height. Operations Research, as an inter-disciplinary approach to problem-solving, developed strategies and tactics which were successfully applied in the war. Today, Operations Research is in the forefront of a different battle – the fight against AIDS. The British OR Society, which has just celebrated its 50th anniversary, has recently formed a special group to apply OR methodology in this new area of threat to mankind.

I would like to thank the editor, authors and sponsors who have worked so hard to bring this book to fruition and I wish them every success in their enterprise.

Frederick J Ridgway
Assistant General Manager
Management Services, Bank of Ireland

ix

THE CONTRIBUTORS

EDITOR

Julian MacAirt, Ph.D., is a graduate of UCC. As a research student, he was awarded a Dunlop Fellowship in Economics at Oxford University. From 1965-67, he worked with Aer Lingus as a market research analyst. He is currently Senior Lecturer in Statistics at Trinity College Dublin (TCD) and a Council member of ORMSI.

CONTRIBUTORS

Frank Bannister is currently a management consultant with Price Waterhouse Informatics. He is a former President of ORMSI and in 1984 represented Ireland at the triennial IFORS conference in Washington, DC. An external lecturer in financial modelling at TCD, he has written and lectured extensively in Decision Support Systems and Modelling.

John Cantwell, an M.A. graduate from Lancaster University, was assigned to OR work in the Government Department of Finance in 1967, where he was in charge of the OR Section until 1978. Thereafter, he was transferred to the Department of Economic Planning and Development. He is currently in the Department of An Taoiseach.

Tom Conlon, a graduate of UCD with an M.Sc. from TCD, is currently Head of Special Projects in the OR Department of the Bank of Ireland. A former President of ORMSI, he presented a paper on *Visual Interactive Modelling* to IFORS in 1984.

Martin Flinter, M.Sc., M.B.A., a graduate of UCD, joined the OR Unit of Aer Lingus in 1967 and branched into General Management Consultancy in 1977 within the airline and ancillary companies. He joined the Marketing Department in 1983, becoming Manager of Product Development in 1984.

Roy Johnston, Ph.D., was a founder member of ORMSI in 1964. Since 1970, he has been working in broad-spectrum applied scientific consultancy at the university/industry interface. His current interests include support for the high-technology enterprise development process at the fringe of the third-level system; international linkage development between growing high-technology firms; and appropriate technology transfer and technological innovation in a Third World context.

Bob Kavanagh, a graduate of UCG, was formerly a lecturer at Birmingham University, Sussex Polytechnic and TCD. Currently, he is Head of the Mathematics Department at the Swinburne Institute in Melbourne, Australia. In 1986, he was elected Vice-President of IFORS.

Richard Kavanagh, Ph.D., has worked in the OR Section of the Department of the Public Service (1972-78); Energy Division of the National Board for Science and Technology (1978-81); Research and Development Directorate, International Energy Agency, Paris (1981-84); and Research and Development Manager, Bord na Móna (1984 to date). Currently, he is President of ORMSI.

Francis Neelamkavil, Ph.D., Senior Lecturer in Computer Science at TCD, has published several papers on optimisation, modelling, simulation and computer-aided design. His book *Computer simulation and modelling* was published by Wiley in 1986. He was elected a Fellow of TCD in 1987.

Seamus O'Carroll, M.B.A., is currently General Manager – Planning with Cement-Roadstone Holdings, having held a number of other positions within the company, including Group Computer Services Manager. Previously, he worked with Aer Lingus in several capacities, including Head of OR. He was President of ORMSI in 1975.

Miceál Ross, Ph.D., is currently Senior Research Officer at the Economic and Social Research Institute. He has published widely in the fields of regional economics, employment and agriculture. He was editor of the Proceedings of the VI IFORS Conference, held in Dublin in 1972.

ACKNOWLEDGEMENTS

The editor sincerely thanks the following individuals for their help and support throughout the compilation of this book: Mrs M Brady; Prof E Cahill, UCC; Mr R Crotty, TCD; Mr N Dingle; Dr P J Drudy, TCD; Mr D Gannon; Mr Bob Kavanagh; Mr E Kelly, Seychelles Tourist Board; Mr B Lenehan, Department of Finance; Mr A Matthews, TCD; Mrs C McClean, Bord Telecom Éireann; Mr B McSweeney, Irish School of Ecumenics; Mr D Nunan, UCC; Ms E Ní Chuilleanáis, TCD; Mr S Ó Buachalla, TCD; Col A O'Byrne; Mr S Ó Cinnéide, Maynooth; Prof J O'Hagan, TCD; Mrs B Walsh – and not least the painstaking and considerate staff of The Mercier Press.

CHAPTER 1

Introduction

BOB KAVANAGH

Swinburne Institute, Melbourne, Australia

The idea for this book came from the Council of the Operations Research and Management Science Society of Ireland (ORMSI) in 1985. It was generally felt that a book describing the development of Operations Research (OR) in Ireland would be a useful addition to existing literature in the field and also be a helpful source of information for students of the subject.

The book aims to achieve two objectives. Firstly, we wanted to provide a book that was easily readable by OR and non-OR people alike. And secondly, we sought to have a representative cross-section of authors from those involved in OR in Ireland over the past two decades. The reader will be the judge of the first; one worry we had regarding this was the variation in style between the authors, but we felt that to make them all conform to a particular style would take greatly from their contributions; hence we have left each, basically, in its original form. With regard to the second objective, we believe these authors represent the OR world in Ireland.

Each chapter has two main ingredients – an historical perspective, followed by a selection of case studies. It is hoped that this book will serve as an appetiser for more detailed case-study discussion, both in the academic and business worlds.

To add extra flavour to the book, interviews were conducted with two of the most eminent OR figures in Ireland – Fred Ridgway (Assistant General Manager of the Bank of Ireland) and David Kennedy (Chief Executive of Aer Lingus).

Fred Ridgway joined the Bank of Ireland in 1967, having previously worked abroad and in Irish industry. He became the manager of the Bank's OR group, which was formed on the recommendation of the management consultants McKinsey. Ridgway was aware that the climate was receptive for OR and it was imperative to meet these expectations. A good first project can be a real blessing to a fledgling OR group and Ridgway, now joined by Terry Forsyth and Pat McGorrian, landed just that in the shape of a modelling of the Bank's lending system. The group developed the idea of changing the Bank's lending system to term lending, whereas up to then the Irish banks lent mainly by the overdraft system. The full recommendations of the OR study were accepted and, in fact, all the Irish clearing banks changed to the new lending system.

The group's first project was, thus, in a vital strategic area. The full impact of the work can best be judged in historical perspective by an account given in the *Irish Banking Review* (Autumn 1986), in which Padraig McGowan (Central Bank of Ireland) wrote, 'A major innovation in bank lending techniques occurred in 1972. The Associated Banks introduced a system of term lending with variable rates of interest which, within a period of about three years, resulted in half of the overdrafts outstanding being converted to term loans.' (Further details of OR work at the Bank of Ireland are given by Tom Conlon in Chapter 4.)

Ridgway has played a major role in the development of OR in Ireland. In 1972, he was Conference Chairman of IFORS VI Triennial Conference, held in Trinity College Dublin (TCD). He has been active in the European Working Group in OR in Banking and Finance. In recent years, he has moved from OR to take responsibility for management services in the Bank of Ireland. Currently, he is Vice-President of the International Federation of Operations Research Societies (IFORS), with responsibility for the Plans and Programmes Committee.

David Kennedy joined Aer Lingus in 1962 as an Operations Research analyst. He was sent to study at the Case Institute of Technology in the USA under Russell Ackoff, where Kevin O'Donnell (up to recently Chief Executive of the New Ireland Assurance Co) was also a student. Kennedy visited Philip Morse (then IFORS Secretary) and, on his return, was encouraged to set up the Operations Research Society of Ireland in 1964, with 20 founder members including Roy Geary (then Director, Economic Research Institute), Donal McCarthy (then Director, Statistics Office), Michael McNamara (Stokes Kennedy and Crowley) and Finbarr Donovan (then Systems Manager, Aer Lingus). The Society's first officers were John Hyland as President, David Kennedy as Secretary and Kevin O'Donnell as Treasurer. Kennedy gave the first paper, on traffic forecasting, at the Economic Research Institute's offices under the chairmanship of Dr Geary.

From 1962-66, Kennedy was an OR analyst for Aer Lingus, working on various projects including exponential smoothing and econometric models for traffic forecasts. With Maurice Foley (who did most of the work), he investigated inventory control of spare parts. From his study of queueing models, to assess staff numbers for telephone reservations and ticket-buying at booking offices, Aer Lingus introduced the quality standard – that 90 per cent of all telephone calls should be answered within 20 seconds.

With Eddie O'Brien, Kennedy worked on a Monte Carlo simulation to forecast effects of changing schedules on punctuality of operations. Another study involved planning some aspects of the real-time reservations system; here, Roy Johnston produced extremely useful theoretical work on where bottlenecks would arise in the computer system. Finally, Kennedy worked on the rostering of pilots and how best to optimise the number of flight crew needed to operate a particular schedule.

AGIFORS, the Airline Group of IFORS, was set up in 1961 and Kennedy hosted the 1966 meeting in Killarney. Air Canada and British European Airways played a large part in this forum, which was useful for informal exchange about common problems.

In 1966, Kennedy became Systems Manager of Aer Lingus. In 1969, he made a presentation on behalf of ORSI to the Venice meeting of IFORS, which led to the 1972 meeting coming to Dublin. During 1970, he worked on Aer Lingus' new programme of ancillary activities and in 1971 moved to New York on becoming Senior Vice-President of the company. OR in the airline developed close links with systems/DP and with methods and work-study, and eventually the name of the OR Unit was changed to 'Organisation Services'. Kennedy became Chief Executive in 1974.

OR people, with their organised approach, training and professional background, have often moved into senior management, both at Aer Lingus and in other airlines. In Kennedy's experience, there is a danger for students of OR to get hung up on mathematics and theory, while the real world cannot be catered for by these. Models should be a means to an end, not an end in themselves. In the real world, OR people must be prepared to consider compromises and qualitative judgements. It is important to involve line departments in the formulation of studies and design of models. (Martin Flinter provides details of OR in Aer Lingus in Chapter 5.)

In Chapter 2, Frank Bannister of Price Waterhouse Informatics deals with the development of financial modelling and gives special attention to the impact of computers on this area of OR. In Chapter 3, John Cantwell of the Department of An Taoiseach describes the birth and development of OR in the Public Service. Their first project was a challenging one – the merger proposed by the Minister for Education between TCD and UCD in 1968. (Having been a lecturer in TCD at the time, I could have predicted the outcome of Cantwell's study – even OR has few answers to academic/political problems.) His other projects give a good insight into the birth and tribulations of a fledgling OR group in the public service.

In Chapter 4, Tom Conlon of the Bank of Ireland gives a brief history of the start of OR and a summary of some applications in the Bank. In Chapter 5, Martin Flinter of Aer Lingus outlines the historical development of OR in that company and provides an account of the type of projects undertaken over the past 25 years.

In Chapter 6, Roy Johnston, Applied Scientific Consultant, summarises 7 OR projects by TCD students during the period 1970-73. In Chapter 7, Richard Kavanagh of Bord na Móna describes the history and development of energy models and their applications. In Chapter 8, Francis Neelamkavil of TCD gives a detailed account of the use of simulation models with the input of computer hardware and software. In Chapter 9,

Seamus O'Carroll of Cement-Roadstone discusses an approach to inflation and cash flow, with appropriate models. Finally, Miceál Ross of ESRI reflects on the history of the ORMSI and the characters involved.

The appendices deal with various aspects of the development of OR in Ireland, such as undergraduate and post-graduate courses and published research carried out in Third-level institutions.

CHAPTER 2

The development of financial modelling in Ireland

FRANK BANNISTER

Price Waterhouse Informatics

Of all the technologies that during the 1960s came under the heading of Operations Research (OR), the one which has made the greatest direct impact – at least in terms of extent of use in Ireland – has been financial modelling.

The reasons for this are easy to understand. Almost every manager in any organisation who has to deal with money sooner or later builds a financial model – even though many of them are written on the backs of envelopes. The use of money to represent a company or organisation is, as the more arcane accountancy text books point out, essentially a modelling activity. The Profit and Loss statement and the Balance Sheet are only models of the company they represent. Add a computer and before you can say 'simultaneous equations' you are into OR – or almost, because one of the ongoing thorny problems of financial modelling is the definition of the term. Much so-called financial modelling is little more than the use of the computer to carry out routine financial mathematical calculations (such as rates of return).

In the author's definition, a model becomes a genuine model when it simulates a real situation and when it is used to explore alternative courses of action. By this definition, much financial modelling is genuine modelling – even if relatively simple by the standards of the more complex areas of mathematical modelling.

It is important for the reader to be clear on one thing. Most, though by no means all, of the financial modelling carried out in Ireland today and over the past twenty years has been of the type known technically as 'discrete time deterministic'. Roughly translated this means that most financial models use fixed and discrete time periods (months, years, etc) and, given the same set of assumptions, will always churn out the same answer. They are also predominantly built on financial and accounting rather than statistical relationships. They are therefore very different from, on the one hand, a Monte Carlo simulation or, on the other, from the econometric models of the type used by, say, the Central Bank.

This is an important distinction and it accounts for why this type of modelling has been so successful in Ireland (as elsewhere) at the expense of more sophisticated techniques. This high level of acceptability is a direct consequence of the fact that users generally understand this type of modelling. They may not necessarily understand how the model is programmed or even know how specialised parts of the model work. But they do understand the concepts on which it is built and this gives them confidence to use it.

However, before considering the use of financial modelling in Ireland today and into the future, it is worthwhile looking over its evolution.

THE EARLY YEARS

Unlike other branches of OR which have more or less continuously evolved (or in some cases failed to evolve) over the past twenty years, financial modelling has undergone a genuine revolution within the past decade. Financial modelling can be divided into the pre- and post-VisiCalc eras. Pre-VisiCalc, there were, of course, users who developed their own models. However, it was only with the launch of VisiCalc that most users found a computer tool to which they could easily relate. In this, Ireland has followed the trend elsewhere. However, in the development of pre-VisiCalc models the Irish OR profession does have a remarkably good record.

The early history of financial modelling in Ireland is very much the story of a number of pioneering organisations and individuals. A small number of names, people, packages and companies dominated the scene. The earliest modelling activities in Ireland were led by Denis Fitzgibbon whose computer bureau (called, with great originality, Time Sharing Ltd) offered ORACLE, a modelling package, which, although fairly primitive by today's standards, was very sophisticated at the time. Unfortunately for its promoters, ORACLE appears to have been too far ahead of its time in that Irish management had, at that point, not yet come fully alive to the possibilities of modelling. Nonetheless, there were many successful ORACLE models built.

While the home-based bureaux, such as Time Sharing Ltd, offered various products, international companies were also muscling in on this emerging market. Honeywell (later GEISCO), with its huge US-based computers, was able to offer computing power and a range of software far greater than its local competitors. IBM also offered the CALL 360 service (where *did* they get the name?), which never seems to have had the same success as the GEISCO system – possibly due to the necessity to dial a UK number to access it. All of this computer power came at a price, of course, and financial modelling therefore tended, in these early years, to be restricted to the rich or the brave. Then, as now, good financial models were worth many times their development cost to management. But, for many managers unused to the concept of modelling as a decision aid, the costs seemed inordinate.

The international time-sharing bureaux also offered an expanding range of modelling tools. In the early 1970s, Price Waterhouse had started to develop a home-grown multi-dimensional modelling system called the PW Business Planning System on the GEISCO time-sharing service. GEISCO themselves had developed a product called TABOL, which was to be highly successful for a time until it was superseded by cheaper minicomputer packages. IBM offered Application System.

The reasons for the success of the bureau-based systems in this area reflects the computing trends of the time. Financial models require powerful (though not necessarily large) computers and in the early 1970s few Irish companies could afford such luxuries. Speed of response is also important. The gap was therefore filled by the computer bureaux who could provide machines sufficiently large to handle the calculations and fast enough to give, if not an instantaneous answer, at least one quick enough to take any remedial action indicated.

THE MINICOMPUTER BOOM

The minicomputer boom in the mid-'70s was followed by a modelling software boom trailing in its wake. By this time, bureaux costs, fuelled by inflation, were going through the roof; costs of several thousand pounds a month were not unusual for a heavily used model. Although the bureaux were vulnerable to minicomputer-based systems, users found that models tended to devour minicomputers for breakfast and the packages were not therefore as successful in displacing the bureaux as might have been expected. Nonetheless, the migration to minicomputers was joined by a new generation of modellers no longer intimidated by potentially huge running costs. Much of the 'modelling' at this time was relatively simple in nature, but it was performing an important and pervasive educational function.

In Ireland, a number of users had also been 'growing their own'. In the early 1970s purchasable packages were few. For ICL users, the ubiquitous PROSPER offered a range of facilities in many ways ahead of its time. (PROSPER failed to develop and eventually lost its lead to more friendly packages.) IBM offered PLANCODE which failed to impress the market. Packages such as FCS and FINAR were yet to become widely available. In the absence of modelling languages on affordable computers, as elsewhere, many early in-house models were built in conventional languages, mainly FORTRAN and later BASIC.

From these in-house projects a number of modelling packages were to develop. In NET, the semi-state fertiliser company, Patrick O'Beirne developed a modelling system called (in what must be one of the worst puns in the business) PROPHET. In 1979, Applied Management Systems launched INSIGHT – a system-34 based package which, while relatively unrefined as a modelling tool, sold so well that it eventually gave its name to the company. While INSIGHT modelling was a long way from OR, it at least had the virtue of increasing middle management awareness of the use of modelling systems. INSIGHT has gone on to win several major software awards, with sales recently topping US $10 million.

AN ERA OF REAL MODELS

By the late 1970s modelling was really on the move, literally as well as metaphorically, in Ireland. Virtually every minicomputer on the market now had a choice of modelling languages available on it and many companies were starting to develop substantial in-house systems.

It is tempting to say that, during this period, models were real models. Some impressive and effective models were built. Financial modelling was now in regular use in all areas of the Irish economy. It would be impossible to list all the applications developed at this time but a few examples will give a cross-section of some of the most exciting work undertaken.

In the semi-state sector, NET built a large model to examine the effect of various pricing structures for the natural gas supplies it would be receiving from the newly discovered Kinsale gas head. The Industrial Development Authority (IDA), with assistance from Price Waterhouse, built a highly sophisticated project evaluation model which enabled the IDA to analyse proposed investments in Ireland by overseas companies.

In the central Civil Service, financial models were used in a variety of tasks including assisting in the key area of negotiating national wage agreements.

In the private industrial sector, a number of companies had been involved in modelling over many years. Cement-Roadstone, the largest construction company in Ireland, had used models from the early 1970s for a wide range of activities – from corporate planning and consolidation to acquisition evaluation. Cantrell and Cochrane, the leading Irish soft-drinks manufacturers, developed an advanced budgeting modelling system which integrated production planning, budget planning and accounting systems. Many other Irish companies were by now using modelling routinely for corporate planning.

In the major banks, models of the 'financial mathematics' type were extensively used for routine calculations. Given that money is their trade this is not surprising, but some of the applications were interesting for technical as well as business reasons. In the Bank of Ireland models were built for lease analysis and other technical areas. Allied Irish Banks also used models for corporate planning and evaluation. Both banks are currently developing their expert systems area as a direct evolution of their financial modelling work.

In agriculture, several of the co-operatives were using financial modelling for a variety of tasks. From the mid-'70s, Waterford Co-Op was using models for allocating milk intake and costs to products. In Kerry Co-Op, modelling had been used extensively in the late 1970s and early 1980s using PROSPER. This was followed by a major FCS-based budgeting and costing model in the early 1980s, which must represent one of the most comprehensive dairy-industry models in Europe.

THE VISICALC REVOLUTION

The advent of VisiCalc in 1979 was the modelling equivalent of the 'big bang' in the financial world. Up to VisiCalc, most modelling languages displayed their third generation roots. By looking at models as spreadsheets rather than conventional computer programs designed to handle tabular data, VisiCalc overcame, in one bound, the enormous comprehension gap that many managers had with financial modelling. Ireland produced its own crop of experts, including Dr T O'Donovan in UCC (*see Appendix D*).[1]

As is so often the case in history, the revolutionaries failed to reap the ultimate benefits of their revolution. Although the inventors of VisiCalc did quite nicely out of their brainchild, it was left to others to really capitalise on the boom in spreadsheets. The leader to date in this race is Lotus Development Corporation's 123. Interestingly enough, Lotus Development Corporation established its European headquarters in Ireland in 1984.

It is unlikely that VisiCalc in itself would have made the dramatic impact it did without the coincidental development of the microcomputer. Even today, mainframe-based spreadsheets are poor and little used by comparison with their microcomputer equivalents. However, in conjunction with the Apple II, VisiCalc brought financial modelling to the masses.

More seriously for the professional financial modellers in Ireland, the availability of end-user computing tools has had a subtle but corrosive effect on the 'modelling' nature of the business. While the construction of models was a black art, the designers and programmers of models could influence the nature of the models themselves to a much greater degree. With users getting in on the act, the trend towards a level of programming simplicity that they could understand meant that it was difficult to sell sophisticated models. Ironically, for all the super software now available the models themselves tended to become paler, if bigger, shadows of their ancestors.

Added to this has been the problem of maintaining model quality. One of the risks of home-made modelling is home-made mistakes. Over the past two years, stories have been leaking out of an increasing number of spreadsheet-instigated disasters abroad. Ireland has yet to have a publicly acknowledged incident of this kind, although the laws of probability dictate that such an event is inevitable sooner or later.

THE CURRENT SCENE

In 1981, the focus of interest in the development of modelling languages again shifted to the mainframe modelling languages with the announcement by Comshare of the Wizard (later System W) decision-support system. Wizard is, in its own way, as revolutionary as VisiCalc was. Unlike its predecessors, Wizard's genuinely non-procedural approach to modelling gave, to those users willing to learn the language and with access to sufficiently powerful computers, the potential to build very sophisticated models without having a doctorate in programming.

Wizard also posed an interesting philosophical question. Based as it is on the computer recognising and resolving non-explicit dependencies in the model, it effectively takes much of the technical programming specification out of the user's hands. This is a great relief to the user, but it does raise the question of how much one can trust what the computer is doing. This is likely to become an increasingly pressing issue over the next few years.

THE FUTURE

The nature of modelling tends to follow the business fashions and problems of the age. For example, during the mid-1970s with high inflation, planning and accounting became a nightmare and models capable of handling the hair-raising complexity of inflation accounting became common. Today, areas such as multidimensional modelling, treasury management and taxation modelling are some of the trends. Many financial modellers have become interested in expert systems as a logical extension of their skills.

With the widespread use of financial modelling has also come user awareness and ambition. Many users have now begun to push spreadsheets to limits to which they were never intended to go. This is leading many people to look, in the words of one supplier, 'beyond the spreadsheet'. One would like to think that the future will also lead to more multidimensional modelling, more use of econometric or statistical methods – more 'real' modelling in fact. As a result of the growth in user knowledge, there may well be a reawakened user-driven interest in 'real' modelling over the next few years. Eventually, the manager who does not use modelling of some sort will probably become the exception rather than the rule. As financial modelling is the most common form of modelling in Ireland, it will happen in this field first.

Although financial modelling is rapidly becoming part of the scenery in Irish management today, there is still a surprisingly large number of Irish companies who have yet to take up modelling in a serious way or realise the potential that it has for helping management decisions. But the faith is spreading rapidly. This is one OR technology that can only continue to expand.

CHAPTER 3

Operations Research in the Public Service in Ireland

JOHN CANTWELL*

Department of An Taoiseach

Following a symposium sponsored jointly by the Irish Government and Organisation for Economic Co-operation and Development, which was held in Dublin in the autumn of 1965, it was decided to form an Operations Research Section in the Irish Public Service. The role of the Section was defined as 'to apply and promote the use of Operations Research as an aid to decision-making at all levels in Government departments and related agencies'.

As the OR Section would service all departments, it was located in the Department of Finance. It was later transferred to the Department of the Public Service when that department was formed in 1973. It was agreed that OR expertise should be concentrated in one unit at the centre, rather than dispersed among different departments. It was considered that this would allow the most effective use of scarce skills and enable a central pool of expertise to be developed. It is also worth noting that the OR Section was set up as a separate independent section and not as an adjunct to computers or organisation and methods.

Staffing the OR Section and getting OR under way presented a difficult but not an unique problem. Different approaches had been suggested, for example by Rivett and Ackoff[1], each approach depending on the circumstances involved. In our case, the strategy adopted was to select two people from within the ranks of the Civil Service who were considered to be suitable material and to possess the right sort

* The views expressed in this paper are the personal responsibility of the author and not necessarily those of the departments in which he served.

of qualifications for OR. These officers were sent abroad for post-graduate training, one to the UK (Lancaster University) and the other to the US (Ohio State University). At that time there were no courses in OR available in Ireland. While these analysts were being trained, the ground was prepared at home. Some senior administrators attended appreciation courses in OR and a short list of possible projects was prepared. Consultants were called in to help get the OR effort off to a good start when the trained analysts returned.

FIRST PROJECTS

The first project was concerned with the proposed merger of the two universities in Dublin – Trinity College Dublin (TCD) and University College Dublin (UCD). The idea of the merger was to eliminate unnecessary duplication between the two colleges, and yet for each to retain the character of a university, with an acceptable spread of subjects. The position was made more complex by the fact that the two universities were on separate sites about 4 miles apart. TCD is in the heart of Dublin city on a confined space, while UCD was being relocated outside the city on a new site with adequate space for expansion.

A small group was formed within the Department of Education to carry forward the implementation of the merger proposals. The OR Section was asked to help this group in their consideration of the allocation of faculties between the two colleges. There were different opinions about which faculties should be amalgamated and put on one site and which should be duplicated on each site. It was agreed that the OR Section would attempt to clarify the issue by developing a model which would show the implications in terms of some agreed criteria of alternative allocations of faculties between the two sites. A model was developed which used as a measure of performance a 'social cost', calculated as the number of student hours which would be lost by students travelling from one site to the other depending on how the faculties were allocated. By using the model it was possible to allocate faculties to sites in such a way as to minimise the 'social cost'. A second stage of the model was envisaged which would take account of capital and current costs of various alternative allocations, but in the event, this stage was not reached.

Before the models were fully developed, it became necessary to make decisions which, in effect, pre-empted the results of the OR study. From the OR point of view, therefore, the project was a failure, insofar as the OR analysis did not impinge directly on the decision. A close look at the reasons for the failure revealed that:

- a proper consultant/client relationship had not been established with the group in the Department of Education;
- the role the OR team would play and the contribution it would make had not been clarified sufficiently at an early stage;
- the group in the Department of Education had not been involved to a sufficient degree in the OR study and did not appreciate what the OR Section was trying to do. In other words, the essential team effort of client and OR analyst did not develop;
- the OR team was not geared to solve the problem in the time allowed.

In effect, most of the mistakes revolved around the interpersonal problems of conducting an OR study and had nothing to do with the technical problems involved. However, management was tolerant and the OR Section was given a second chance.

Before going on to describe the second chance, I would like to suggest that although OR groups are advised to take on well-defined classic OR type problems to start with, the pressure to go for 'the big one', particularly if the opportunity presents itself, is overwhelming. It would be a very conservative OR group who would pass up such an opportunity. Perhaps the answer is to try to steer management away from asking the group to become involved in difficult macro problems until the unit feels confident to tackle them. There is, on the other hand, the danger that if the OR group insists on tackling low-level well-defined problems to start with and succeeds in building up a reputation for competence in this area, it may find it difficult to elevate its work and break into higher ground later.

The best approach to adopt depends to a large extent on the experience of the analysts and the degree to which they are familiar with the organisation. Their relative seniority, both in age and stature within the organisation, should also be considered. Harvey Shycon, writing in *Interfaces* in August 1972, suggests four stages:[2]

- small sub-projects to begin with;
- a full-scale project covering an important functional area;
- this followed by further smaller projects;
- a conscious move into a major planning project of top management significance.

This is, undoubtedly, a good approach, but it should be used with discretion and at all times made subject to management's requirements.

A SECOND CHANCE

The guidelines set out above were not adhered to in the case of the OR Section's first project. The next project was again of major top management significance. In 1968, there had been a fall-off in the inflow of money into National Savings. The OR Section was asked to examine this problem and to advise on how National Savings might be made more attractive. This time the Section, which still consisted of two analysts, was on its own and consultants were not called in.

A considerable amount of analysis was carried out to determine the effect of changes in, for example, interest rates and tax concessions on savers' habits. Definite relationships were difficult to identify, but it was evident that interest rates were not the overriding consideration. Data from the Post Office Savings Bank were analysed in detail to discover the behaviour pattern of investors. Some of the most interesting findings in this area were that:

- small savers tended to save enthusiastically when they joined the movement first, but after about 18 months their enthusiasm waned and they gradually began to withdraw their savings;
- there was a net withdrawal from old accounts and a net inflow into new accounts.

These and other findings pointed to the need for a regular instalment type of saving scheme. A saving scheme on these lines (National Instalment Saving) was introduced shortly after the OR study had been completed, but although OR had an input the decision was not made solely as a result of the OR analysis.

The Savings study was slightly more successful than the Merger study, but it was not an unqualified success. Again, there was a lack of problem definition and management involvement, and the tendency to go away, work on the problem and come back with the answers was still very strong.

It should be obvious to all OR analysts that they do not simply write a report as they might write a doctoral thesis and then post it to the sponsors. They will not be impressed; in fact I doubt if they would take the trouble to read it. Writing a report and presenting the results deserve a lot of attention; indeed, competence in this area is vital if recommendations arising out of OR studies are to be implemented. We have found it very important to produce clear and concise reports, but perhaps in the civil service people are conditioned to expect readable documents which are then circulated for observations.

Implementation also depends to a large extent on how a study is conducted. A satisfactory relationship between analyst and client must be established from the beginning. The analyst must work to develop confidence in the client and to encourage an analyst/client team approach to the problem. The client is not interested in sophisticated mathematical techniques; he is interested only in his problem and in having it solved. If OR studies were conducted properly at the interpersonal level, there would be fewer problems with implementation. Part of the trouble in this area can also be attributed to a failure to follow-through and stick with the study to the end. OR groups usually consist of highly qualified research-orientated people who delight in intellectual challenge. When a problem has been solved to their own personal intellectual satisfaction, they can often lose interest and become restless to tackle something new. This tendency is dangerous. The study is not completed until the client is satisfied and the recommendations are implemented – in other words, in the case of the civil service, until the OR model is embedded into the normal decision-making procedures of the client department.

Even when recommendations have been implemented, the need for follow-up still exists. Recommendations need to be reassessed in the light of current events and updating may require the use of computer programs which the client may not be fully familiar with. This can be a time-consuming task, but it is surely one of the services to be expected from an in-house consultancy group.

A WELL-DEFINED PROBLEM

Although it is desirable to start with a reasonably well-defined project amenable to the OR approach, this may not be possible for a variety of reasons. Indeed, the OR Section's opportunity to work on such a problem did not come until nearly two years after the unit had been formed.

The problem concerned the operation of the ambulance service in the Western Health Board area. The OR Section was asked to examine the operation of the service and to advise on the number and location of ambulances required to provide a specific level of service in relation to response to emergency calls. This case had all the ingredients of the classic OR problem. It was quantifiable; a large number of alternative strategies relating to the number and location of ambulances were possible; and there was uncertainty about the effect these alternative strategies would have on the level of service.

The study when completed allowed the Health Board to test the effect of different operating policies and to select the most suitable in relation to level of service and cost. The study has since been carried out for most of the health boards in the country and the level of implementation has been good. (A paper based on the study was presented to the IFORS VI Conference held in Dublin in 1972.)

While this study was going on, the OR Section was asked to advise on the number of driver-testers required in each region of the country so that delays in having a driving test would not exceed, say, two months and would be about the same for each region. Here again, there was good problem definition and scope for applying standard OR techniques.

In parallel with such project work, the Section was actively engaged in promoting and encouraging the use of OR. These efforts soon began to pay dividends and in the following five years or so, a great variety of work was carried out, including studies for:

- the Department of Posts and Telegraphs in relation to project co-ordination problems, selective voucher checking systems, inventory management policies, manpower planning and recruitment policies, and financial planning models;
- the Department of Health in relation to hospital bed/population ratios;
- the Department of Education in relation to teacher numbers and costs in colleges of technology;
- the Department of Agriculture in relation to resource allocation at farm level;
- the Department of Justice in relation to police radio networks and replacement policies for patrol cars;
- the Department of the Environment in relation to vehicle replacement policies and the number and location of paved sites for storing road-dressing material;
- the Forest and Wildlife Service in relation to fire protection policy in State forests and resource allocation for land purchase, preparation and planting.

PROMOTING OPERATIONS RESEARCH

An OR group if it wishes to be successful cannot afford to sit back and wait for projects to roll in. It must pursue an active promotion policy. This promotion policy must aim primarily at establishing confidence in the prospective clients. The gap between the client's view of the problems and what the OR group has to offer must be bridged. This will not be achieved by talking in technical terms about OR and quoting text-book examples, but rather by discussing actual case studies relevant to the manager's own area of responsibility. An OR unit should try to avoid adding its voice to the babble of management advisers who, by peddling their various wares, tend to confuse rather than assist.

The OR Section's initial efforts at promotion consisted of two-day appreciation courses for selected groups. The object of these courses was to enable participants to identify (and bring to the notice of the OR Section) problems in their own administrative areas which the OR Section could help with.

These appreciation seminars, which were repeated twice a year for three consecutive years, helped to create an awareness of what the OR Section could do. They were also valuable in helping the OR Section to get a feel for the types of problems facing administrators in different government departments.

A second method which was used to promote OR was to compile a list of five or six possible problems which might face decision-makers in, say, the Department of Health or the Department of Education. These lists were compiled from background reading, from our own general knowledge about the area and from an examination of OR literature. These lists provided background material for discussions with the departments concerned. Usually one or two firm proposals would emerge from these discussions.

The easiest way to promote OR, of course, is to point to a successful record of achievement. When one or two successful studies have been completed progress is easier, but the problem lies in achieving these early successes.

STAFFING THE OR UNIT
Two civil servants, both engineering graduates, were selected to form the nucleus of the OR Section. Two years later, two further graduates were assigned to the Section, which remained at this strength although some changes in personnel occurred.

In the early years, there were two separate entry streams to the Section. Recent graduates were assigned from the general civil service entry stream, or experienced analysts were recruited (or seconded) on short-term contracts. These experienced personnel fulfilled two main needs: they helped to get work done and to train new civil service entrants. They also introduced new ideas and helped the Section compare its progress with other OR groups.

Work was also sub-contracted to consultants and to

universities when necessary. Such work usually involved well-defined self-contained parts of ongoing projects.

CHAPTER 4

Operations Research in the Bank of Ireland

TOM CONLON

Bank of Ireland

BRIEF HISTORY

Operations Research was introduced into the Bank of Ireland in 1967. It was a time of considerable change in banking. Recent mergers had led to the emergence of two major commercial banks of about equal size, the Bank of Ireland and Allied Irish Banks. A process of unification within each group was underway, and management began to change from a very traditional conservative style to a more modern style with functional specialisation. The Bank of Ireland had no computer, not even an electronic calculator, and very few graduates. Its single tier recruitment system had meant that management skills were learned on the job.

After an extensive study of the Bank of Ireland's organisational needs by McKinsey management consultants, the need to form a professional Operations Research Unit within the headquarters was identified. This recommendation was accepted and OR specialists were attracted into the Bank.

Fred Ridgway was recruited to start this Unit. A UCD graduate in experimental physics, he had worked in his early OR days with CIE, the semi-state Irish Transport Company. In 1968 the Unit was joined by Terry Forsyth, a UCD physics graduate who had been working with the UK Local Government OR Unit. Pat McGorrian, a QUB graduate, completed the group.

Their role was not easy, because it took some time to overcome scepticism to the application of the scientific method to management problems. However, it is to the credit of the team that a significant contribution was made to profitability.

Through the late 1960s and 1970s, the Bank established or

expanded all the functions of a modern business organisation with a Computer Department and Management Information Systems, including planning and control. The OR Unit reached a maximum of about 14 staff at one stage. All further graduate recruitment was through the sending of existing Bank staff through a scholarship scheme, which usually meant a Business degree followed by a Statistics/OR postgraduate degree at TCD.

The work first done by the Bank's OR Unit was inherited from the McKinsey study. Most of the projects dealt with major strategic issues, such as costing and pricing of services. During 1983, the OR function was moved to the Operations Area with a brief to concentrate on 'Workplace OR'. This was to deal with the operation of the branch network. The Unit re-examined branch strategy and was responsible for implementing major elements. A new title, Special Projects, came into being and its role was the coming of age of OR.

OR skills are now dispersed through the Bank of Ireland. Ridgway currently heads the Management Services Section, whose duties include customer and product profitability. McGorrian is Group Treasury Manager, heading the team responsible for the Gilt-edged Investment Section. Forsyth is head of Research and Development in Personnel, with responsibility for personnel research, planning, recruitment and pensions. The author is head of Special Projects in the Operations Department.

MAJOR DEVELOPMENTS

Term lending: The first task for OR was to reorganise the lending structure. Up to then the Bank had usually lent money by overdraft, which had problems of control both at individual customer level and in managing the Bank's overall liquidity. It was basically a short-term lending instrument, whereas major business and personal customers needed medium-term finance. Developing an alternative to overdraft-lending involved major surveys and modelling of the effects on both Bank and customer, leading to the term-lending system, started around 1970 and which still exists today.

Manpower planning: In a highly labour-intensive organisation with a single tier of recruitment, manpower planning is an important tool of management. Recruitment decisions taken today have implications for many future years. The OR Unit developed its own computer manpower models and helped the personnel function in policy formulation through 'what if?' models. This work raised the appreciation by management as to what OR and computers could do. Forsyth and his staff have now refined the models and are using them to explore staff scenarios based on alternative personnel policies for future years.

Product and customer profitability: Fair and reasonable attribution of costs in a multi-product organisation has been a preoccupation of OR since about 1970. The range of services provided by a bank to meet the needs of a variety of customers is surprisingly extensive. The majority are channelled through an expensive branch network, with elaborate computer and other infrastructural backing. Detailed product and service costing is essential to strategic decision-making, including product development, marketing and pricing.

Earliest experiments in credit scoring date back to 1971. This is a system of discriminating between good and bad potential risks in the personal lending sector, based on features of the customer's application. It depends on a discriminant analysis of recent loan applications. A small system was installed in 1979, but the major method was based on the OR Unit's project of 1985.

During this time, the OR Unit had been experimenting successfully with systems for measuring and simulating activity within the branch environment. These were based on Visual Interactive Modelling (VIM), which presents a simulation in animated form on a coloured screen. This method has proved powerful in analysing customer-behaviour patterns.

Tax-based lending: During the 1970s and 1980s, tax-based lending was used by Government to attract new industrial investment to Ireland. Through leasing, preference shares and 'Section 84' lending, a bank could reduce its tax liability and pass on this benefit to the customer in reduced financing charges. The Bank of Ireland's OR Unit became involved in tax-based lending at account level, developing the systems for making quotations. This required individual planning models to suit major deals, together with a specialised accounting system.

Tax-based lending was the basis of a range of OR projects, becoming more a way of life than a project. Apart from mathematical skills, it was frequently necessary to insert mathematical formulae into legal documents to allow for changes in tax rates or taxation practice, interest rate charges, exchange rates and the other elements making up a transaction.

The allocation models for this were models for an overall 5-year planning model of the spreadsheet type, with a variety of approaches to sensitivity analysis.

ACCOUNT-LEVEL MODELLING

In engaging in sophisticated forms of project financing, such as Section 84 and leasing, a bank is concerned with obtaining an acceptable margin over cost of funds. As margins became tighter due to competition, it was found necessary to insert into major legal documents:

- a liquidity adjustment for the cost of funds, to compensate for obligations on a bank to raise funds in excess of the amount required and to maintain the excess as liquid funds;
- a tax delay adjustment, to compensate for the delay between the passing of benefits to the customer and realisation of those benefits by the bank;
- interest-rate adjustments, to formulate a lease so that the rental responds to prevailing interest rates.

As each improvement of documentation was made by the OR Unit, it became an industry standard, often within weeks. The grapevine of the financial world is very effective. The tax-lending operation required a range of skills – accounting, legal, banking and mathematical. It was a situation where answers were always required yesterday.

COMPUTER SUPPORT SYSTEMS

The Bank's OR Unit has always tried to maintain an independent line on computer systems. The mainframe systems were designed primarily for batch operation to process large volumes of cheques and other paper. Until 1980 the Unit relied on time-sharing systems, first with TCD and later with various external operators, notably GEISCO. After 1980 most of the models were microcomputer-based. This gave the OR Unit a faster turnaround, more independence and access to a wider variety of software.

CHAPTER 5

Operations Research
in Aer Lingus

MARTIN FLINTER

Aer Lingus

The story of Operations Research in Aer Lingus probably goes back at least to the 1950s, when studies which we would now regard as OR were first carried out. However, OR was first formally recognised in 1960 with the employment of the first OR analyst, J J McCool. This review gives a condensed history of Aer Lingus OR over the past 25 years – its development, contribution, problems and future. The author is indebted to a 1967 paper of the same title[1], on the structure and content of which this chapter is liberally based. The case studies reported are based on the work both of the central OR Unit and the Economic Planning Department of Aer Lingus.

AER LINGUS
Aer Lingus is the Irish national airline and operates scheduled and charter services from Ireland to 50 destinations throughout Europe and North America. While small by international standards, it has nevertheless carved out a reputation for itself as a professional, sturdy and progressive airline within the international aviation community. Through its Ancillary Activities Division, it has also left its mark in numerous other fields outside the airline proper, notably in the maintenance of other airline fleets, in hotel management, data processing, recruitment, management contracts for other airlines and hospital management. It is interesting looking back to see the extent to which former OR specialists have been involved in these developments.

The Aer Lingus fleet currently consists of 3 Boeing 747, 14 Boeing 737, 4 BAC 1-11, 4 Shorts 360 and 2 Boeing 737-300.

Annual revenue in 1985-86 stood at £536m, with 2.25 million passengers carried and a reported profit of £16m. This was the highest profit ever recorded and was doubly welcome since 1986 also marked the 50th anniversary of Aer Lingus.

AIRLINE OPERATIONS RESEARCH

The classic definition of OR – as the application of quantitative techniques and scientific method to the solution of management problems – is probably an adequate description of what airline OR specialists do. OR work in Aer Lingus and other airlines satisfying this definition is heavily documented in the annual proceedings of AGIFORS (Airline Group of the International Federation of Operations Research Societies).

However, and perhaps this is also the case outside the airline business, it would be inaccurate and inappropriate to suggest that this is what OR people are doing or are expected to do, all of the time. In the author's experience, OR analysts are expected to be able to assist management in solving virtually any type of management problem. This is probably because managers, having been exposed to OR people, quickly come to see them not just as quantitative technicians but also as useful resources in the more general management consultancy sense. This perception is generally welcomed by the OR practitioner, who sees and is attracted to the wider brief and the opportunities which it presents. Thus, a possibly more apt definition of OR, at least in the Aer Lingus context, is whatever the OR specialist is doing at the time. As a consequence, many OR specialists are encouraged in time to develop outwards within the organisation into line and senior management roles. This phenomenon is evident not just in Aer Lingus but in other airlines as well.[2]

DEVELOPMENT OF OR IN AER LINGUS

Aer Lingus recruited its first OR analyst in 1960. In the years that followed a special section, the OR Unit, was set up which quickly grew to a staff of six. These analysts were additional to a smaller number of management scientists who worked for the Economic Planning Department and concentrated primarily on financial modelling for corporate decision-making. In 1987, the OR Unit had a staff of three analysts and is likely to remain at or about this level in the foreseeable future.

Organisationally, the OR Unit is located in the Management Services Department which is part of the Personnel Division of Aer Lingus. Also within Management Services are other management resource units, such as Organisation Services (organisation and methods, manpower evaluation, etc), Data Processing, Systems and Telecommunications, Training, and Job Evaluation. In many situations it is appropriate to combine two or more of these functions together with user personnel into project teams when addressing today's complex management problems. From the OR analyst's perspective, this is particularly beneficial in helping to broaden his/her concept of the organisation and its workings, so that ultimately OR's potential can be most accurately directed at the real needs of the organisation.

The emphasis of OR in Aer Lingus has changed somewhat in recent years. The nature of the decision processes and the ways in which they can be influenced by OR have developed and broadened. For example the airline planning environment has become more difficult, with increased levels of competition and changes taking place in the public perception of air travel. The tools available to planners have also changed dramatically, with developments in microcomputing and the emergence of 'expert systems' (souped-up versions of some earlier OR models?). All of these forces combine to open up a new era of immense potential and challenge for OR analysts.

In addition, many of the areas of traditional interest to OR in Aer Lingus – inventory control, manpower planning, investment analysis and strategic planning – have in recent times been the subject of new OR studies and existing decision models will continue to be targeted for continual improvement and enhancement in the years ahead.

Since the early 1960s, much OR work has been carried out in Aer Lingus. Some case studies are discussed below; they are by no means comprehensive and perhaps concentrate on classical type OR work rather than on the much broader range of activities in which OR specialists have been involved.

CASE STUDY: INVENTORY OR STOCK CONTROL

One of the major airline problems tackled in the early years of OR in Aer Lingus was that of inventory or stock control. In very approximate terms, the airline's holding of technical spares (excluding spare engines) is in excess of £30m, spread over almost 200,000 parts.

With this level of investment, effective management of spares is given a high priority. However, management of airline spares poses a series of unique and difficult problems, such as:

- very high potential shortage costs (e.g. aircraft grounded);
- very long and variable lead times on many parts (can be 12 months and longer on occasion);
- highly irregular or infrequent demand;
- very high volume of parts;
- need to make significant initial investment in spares for new aircraft types before any worthwhile experience has been developed;
- large associated holding costs due to high unit costs, slow turnover and risk of obsolescence.

The earlier OR work in this area focused on the class of inventory items known as consumables (expendables).[3] Two independent models were developed, one for what we in Aer Lingus term 'fast-moving parts' (5 or more units consumed per annum) and the second for 'slow-moving parts' (demand of 4 or less units per annum, typically with a high unit and shortage cost).

In neither case did the classical inventory approach, of minimising the combination of holding, ordering and shortage cost, apply (*below*). The classical questions – how much to order (ROQ) and when to order (ROL) – thankfully did apply. The main problem with the classical Wilson formula[4] was that the level of ordering required would have outstripped the capacity of the administration system by a factor of at least 2:1 and this was with the advantage of a sophisticated (for the 1960s) computerised inventory management system which was being installed at the same time. In this context the concept of a constant marginal order cost goes out the window and is replaced by a high stepping cost function as extra staff are injected to handle the increased workload.

The second biggest problem in adhering to the classical approach was the assumption that management desired a minimum cost solution *ab initio*. In fact, management's prime requirement was for a solution that would function operationally from day one and which, in principle at least, could be moved towards the lowest cost optimum over time – that is, the system would serve management within the global corporate objectives rather than management serving the system.

The problem, therefore, was to devise a model which would keep the overall level of ordering more or less fixed, while maintaining an acceptable level of service to the airline's main function – flying airplanes. Within these constraints (which could be varied by management discretion after a fashion), the objective was the classical one of minimising inventory costs. This reduction was to be achieved by allocating a fixed number of orders over the range of parts in such a way that the level of ordering on a part was proportional to the square-root of the value of annual turnover for that part. Analogous, though more complex rules were developed, producing ROLs as a function of price – that is, the higher the price, the more likely the part fulfills a critical function, thus implying a higher shortage cost.

For slow-moving parts, the approach taken was to assume that demand was for one unit at a time and that all demands result in an order for one replacement unit. The problem was to determine re-order level ROL as a function of demand, cost, lead time and shortage cost (including risk of obsolescence). In other words, should the ROL be 0, 1, 2, 3 or 4? The solution was based on work carried out by Mitchell[5] into slow-moving engineering spares and has served Aer Lingus well over the years.

Following implementation, these models produced improvements in stock turnover ratios of the order of 30 per cent, while maintaining previous order and stockout rates. However, with the passage of time the models gradually fell into disuse with regard to some of the relatively slow-moving (classified in the model as fast-moving) critical parts. While the reasons for this are many and varied and not all related to the effectiveness of the models, the author's view is that the main reason was a deficiency in systems design in the first instance and a failure by management to react swiftly enough in the second. The design deficiency was in the process of feeding the model with consumption forecasts and in the lack of adequate system facilities to monitor their efficacy. Specifically, the system maintains a four-year consumption history on each part for forecasting purposes, but leaves the task of inputting consumption estimates (on which ROQ and ROLs are based) to the spares-planner. (The pain experienced by a planner in the event of a stockout on a critical part can be of a far higher order than the shortage cost assumed by the model and human nature being what it is, one cannot altogether blame the planner.)

Other shortcomings of the original model were also being identified around this time, such as in the area of forecasting techniques, and a range of possible improvements was emerging.[6] In the mid-1970s, management was torn between fixing the system (not so much in terms of wresting control from the planner, who in the final analysis must carry the can, but rather to build in a monitoring of performance) at considerable expense or replacing it with an entirely new maintenance and engineering system capable of meeting the needs of the airline into the '80s and '90s. In the event, management took the latter course and is now well down the road to introducing one of the most advanced systems of its kind to be found in aviation today.[7]

With the new online system, one of the key constraints in the original model is removed in one stroke – capacity to place orders is now virtually unlimited. Reorder quantities can now be based on standard application of the Wilson formula. Service levels, by part or range of parts, will take the place of shortage costs as the determinant of reorder levels. Consumption forecasts using exponential smoothing will be used to assist the planner. The planner still has the final decision and can override the model whenever there is better information. Finally, the system includes provision for sophisticated management-information capabilities.

CASE STUDY: THE TOTAL COMPANY MODEL

In the early days of airline OR, much thought and discussion was given to the possibility of creating a 'Total Company Model' which would be used to guide corporate management in *all* areas of strategic decision-making. While it is possible to conceptualise such a model without too much difficulty, and it should even be beneficial for operations researcher and corporate management alike to make the effort, no-one (so far as the author is aware) has so far managed to go the full distance and develop the 'Total Company Model' for an airline.

In Aer Lingus, a partial solution was found to the 'Total Company' problem with the 'Route Profitability Programme', which was developed within the Economic Planning Department in the mid-to-late 1960s.[8] The model and some of its derivatives are used for a variety of tasks, including the development of five-year financial plans, annual route profitability analyses and economic evaluation of route opportunities.

The basic concepts used in the model evolved from a number of earlier studies concerned with fleet planning, for the transition by Aer Lingus from all-propeller to all-jet operations, and later in the area of capacity planning.[9, 10]

In the route profitability analysis, the model projects annual operating surpluses for the airline, and within this for each individual route and logical route subgroup (such as Ireland-North America, charters, freighters, etc). Profitability is analysed at three levels:

- Surplus 1 (S1): Revenue less direct costs;
- Surplus 2 (S2): Revenue less direct and indirect costs;
- Surplus 3 (S3): Revenue less direct, indirect and overhead costs.

Financial outputs are supplemented by a battery of other performance indicators, such as S3/Rev, breakeven load factors, passenger and cargo yields, and cost per capacity unit.

Direct costs in the model include only genuine additional out-of-pocket costs, such as fuel, airport-handling fees, subcontract costs, crew expenses and maintenance accrual. Crew, airport and maintenance payroll are treated as indirect costs as are aircraft standing charges (insurance, depreciation, etc). Overheads are all other costs including administration, sales, distribution and general overheads.

From the model-builder's perspective, one of the most interesting elements is the method of allocating overhead costs to routes. Due to the highly seasonal nature of Aer Lingus traffic, it is necessary to avoid penalising developmental or marginal operations with an undue proportion of the cost of expensive resources required to service peak operations on established routes. This problem was overcome by developing algorithms which would spread indirect and overhead costs in a realistic manner. For example, aircraft standing charges are spread in proportion to peak aircraft block hours, airport costs in proportion to peak week departures/arrivals, and administration costs by production unit (capacity ton mile).

In today's terms, this is an ideal spreadsheet application of fairly large dimensions. In fact, that is how it was done (on large desk-size sheets of paper) before the computer model was developed. It is a tribute to the workmanship involved in the initial development that the original model (albeit considerably enhanced over the years) is still in use 20 years later. Each year, outputs from the model are analysed, interpreted and bound in a confidential report which is avidly studied and discussed by airline management in the annual planning and review process.

CASE STUDY: MANPOWER PLANNING
A further 'obvious' area in the airline context for the application of OR skills was that of manpower planning. Despite the high level of technology with which aviation is universally associated, airlines are highly manpower-intensive when it comes to handling their prime commodities – aircraft and passengers. The manpower-planning problems for airlines are all the more acute where there are pronounced seasonality patterns to their operations, as is the case in Aer Lingus. Essentially Aer Lingus operates three different schedules in the course of a year: peak (July/August), shoulder (May/June and September/October) and off-peak (November/April). Peak activity is of the order of twice that of the off-peak.

In determining permanent staffing levels in what are called frontline areas, Aer Lingus aims for a happy medium between peak and off-peak requirement. Staff surplus to requirement in the off-peak period are encouraged to take annual and special winter leave, temporary staff are recruited in the run-up to the peak period, and leave for permanent staff is restricted. This topping-up policy does not apply in the case of pilots, due to the problems of finding suitably qualified pilots on the open market in the peak period.

Over the years, OR studies aimed at determining minimum peak manpower requirements were concentrated in 3 main areas: telephone and sales office reservations staff; pilots and cabin crew; and passenger and aircraft handling staff.

The reservations staff was one of the first areas to be studied by the OR Unit.[11] During operating hours, staff are required to handle widely fluctuating volumes of calls either by phone or in person. The length of such calls can also vary considerably, ranging, for example, from a caller who simply wants to confirm a departure time to the caller who wishes to discuss and finalise a family trip to Australia with four stopovers en route. A third passenger standing in line, either physically or electronically, behind the latter might be sorely tempted to give up and try another airline.

In the case of both the telephone and personal caller, the queueing situation can be addressed using standard analytic queueing techniques. As the prime objective of the airline is not to turn away business unreasonably, the question for the model can be phrased somewhat as follows: 'how many servers (staff) are required such that 90 per cent of telephone calls in the peak hour of the peak day are answered within 20 seconds?'

Using empirical data on transaction times, traffic forecasts and historical caller profiles by month, week and day, the detailed hourly manpower requirement is established using the appropriate models. These are then allocated into shifts and rosters based on working agreements and total staffing requirements are determined. In addition to staffing, the models are also used to determine other related resources, such as phone lines, video display units and counter positions.

The second area to be studied by the OR Unit was the

aircrew. Here the problem was usually in the form: 'given the fleet, the schedule and the legal and working constraints on cabin and cockpit crew, what is the minimum number of crew required to satisfy all duties?'

Other constructions are also to be found in the industry, such as minimise the total operating cost and minimise the number of crew duties. The OR approaches used in the industry to solve the general crew-scheduling problem are many and varied, but can usually be classified under one of two headings – mathematical programming or heuristic (rule-of-thumb) methods. Despite considerable research into the problem by Aer Lingus, an acceptable working solution using computer models has yet to be developed.[12] This is because the solutions derived using manual methods always looked close to optimal. Or to put it another way, compared to the larger carriers the potential benefits to Aer Lingus of a fully computerised solution never looked sufficiently enticing to justify the effort involved. The emphasis today is more on providing computer aids to our crew-scheduling staff to assist them in constructing manual rosters, allocating duties, monitoring training needs and managing crew expenses.

The third main area of manpower studies is that of passenger and aircraft handling at the airports where Aer Lingus carries out both its own and other airline handling, namely Dublin, Shannon, Cork, Heathrow, JFK and Boston. In addition to handling its own passengers and aircraft, Aer Lingus provides similar services to other carriers at each of these airports, earning revenues of the order of £20m per annum.

Every time there is a change in either its own or one of its customer airline schedules, there is a corresponding change in manpower required to handle tasks such as check-in, baggage delivery and aircraft servicing.

For check-in type operations, computer models have been developed using standard queueing theory as for reservations, but allowing for more 'lumpy' passenger arrival profiles to be expected in an airport environment. Staff numbers are calculated using minimum service standards set by management.

Apron manpower is determined using heuristic rules which allocate preset numbers of men to aircraft based on aircraft type, length of turnround and services required. Total manpower numbers by type are then calculated for each five-minute interval of the operating day. A process which Aer Lingus call 'peak chopping' is then used to test the sensitivity of peak manpower levels to small variations in aircraft arrival/departure times. Where manpower savings can be achieved with relatively small timing changes these cases are then investigated further with the schedulers concerned.

These models[13] were initially developed in the late 1960s and have undergone considerable refinement and upgrading over the years to reflect the changing environment. Their use has now become an accepted part of the normal routine of agreeing peak and valley manpower requirements between the line functions and senior management; operations research is consulted only when the models need to be modified. With the arrival of the 'micro' and links to the mainframe computer, the latest battery of changes relate to improving the presentation of results and to the ease with which reruns under varying planning assumptions can be accomplished.

PHYSICAL PLANNING

Continued growth and changing behaviour in air travel invariably leads to inadequate or uneconomically sized facilities. In the area of ground facilities management, scientists in Aer Lingus have conducted a number of studies over the years.

Arrivals Terminal: One of the first of these studies was undertaken in 1967 and related to the old arrivals building at Dublin Airport (which now houses the Express Parcel depot run by the Post Office on the lower level and the Aer Lingus Technical Ground Training School on the upper level).[14] The problem at the time was to determine when the Arrivals Building would cease to be large enough to cope with passenger flows. This was against a background where a new Passenger Terminal was planned for Dublin Airport in 1970. Airport management were concerned that the existing terminal would be overloaded before the new terminal came on-stream; if that were the case, management wished to identify whatever interim alterations would help to alleviate the problems.

A computer simulation model was developed using Monte

Carlo techniques. The model was used to monitor and predict the interaction of facilities within the building, with passenger arrival profiles based on aircraft schedules. Passenger queueing times and concentrations (per square foot) were measured at each of the main holding points – immigration, baggage hall, customs clearance and the transit lounge. Responsiveness, in terms of passenger service, to additional manpower and physical resources was also tested using the model. Output from the model was used to assist in decisions to increase the capacity of the existing facility.

Hangar Capacity: Aer Lingus has five aircraft maintenance hangars at Dublin Airport. These are numbered Hangar 1 through 5, reflecting their chronological arrival on the Airport landscape. Their physical size also reflects this, with the largest, Hangar 5, being the only one which can accommodate a B747. The cost of building new hangars is extremely high, necessitating accurate and in-depth analysis of all of the planning parameters involved. In the planning for Hangar 5, this requirement resulted in a computer simulation model being developed by one of our economic planning specialists to assess the long-term requirement for hangar accommodation.[15]

The model assumed that hangar capacity depends on:
- the type of aircraft in operation;
- the number of aircraft of each type;
- the frequency of occurrence of scheduled maintenance checks as generated by flying hours or elapsed time since the previous check;
- the frequency and duration of unscheduled maintenance.

The model also assumed that manpower, equipment and spares are available to meet demand. The planning horizon was taken as five years.

The model spreads the total projected annual flying hours by aircraft type over each aircraft in the fleet in accordance with a given set of rules. It then generates a programme of scheduled maintenance events based on the total flying hours/elapsed time legally allowed between overhauls. Unscheduled maintenance is stochastic in nature and is obtained from historical data using a random procedure. The output from the maintenance model is input to a second model, which attempts to allocate aircraft to service bays in the hangars based on aircraft size and expected service time. This model monitors waiting times and service bay utilisations for a range of operating assumptions.

US Immigration Preclearance: A further opportunity to apply OR technique to a physical planning problem arose quite recently with evaluation of proposals to locate US immigration preclearance facilities at Shannon Airport. The rationale behind the proposals (which are still under evaluation) is to eliminate the queueing delays experienced by international passengers arriving at New York's JFK Airport due principally to slow immigration processing by locating an immigration preclearance facility at Shannon. One of the relevant questions for Aer Lingus was how much faster would its passengers reach the kerbside after arrival at JFK?

To help answer this question, a straightforward simulation model was developed,[16] which modelled the proposed versus the existing situation for non-US passengers disembarking at JFK's International Arrivals Building. Estimates of passenger walking, queueing and service times and their distributions were developed. Passengers were categorised by class of service and by whether they had checked in baggage or hand-baggage only. The model was then able to calculate the time advantage by passenger category.

This was not a very complicated model. However, what is interesting is that it was possible to design, develop, test and implement the model in a matter of a few days, due to the availability of on-line computer power and a well-known statistical simulation package. It is not so long ago that this same exercise would have taken weeks to reach the same stage of development.

REAL-TIME COMPUTER RESERVATIONS SYSTEM

Aer Lingus entered the era of real-time passenger reservations back in 1969 using IBM 360s. From this point onwards, it became possible for an Aer Lingus sales agent in contact with a prospective passenger to directly interrogate and update the computer system from a CRT in a remote location. This meant that the sales agent could request from the terminal seat availability on a particular flight, sell and confirm a seat reservation to the passenger, and insert relevant details, such as passenger name, contact address or phone number and ticket number – and all in real-time. As might be appreciated, the ability to make real-time reservations on-line from remote terminals represented a major technological step forward in the distribution of an airline's primary product – namely seats on airplanes.

In preparation for this step, there was little in the way of previous experience to guide the airline in choosing between the product offerings of alternative computer vendors or indeed in sizing the hardware configuration which would be necessary to handle their reservations activity over the time-span of what would be significant capital and manpower investments. The Aer Lingus team charged with the responsibility of choosing and implementing its system called on in-house Operations Research expertise to assist it in solving some of the problems that arose. Among these were:

- the evaluation of the capability of various proposed configurations to handle the stochastic demand from the sales offices;
- the determination of relationships between the number of agent sets needed and the passenger call volumes and related service standards in the various sales offices.

The first of these problems is discussed here. A real-time reservations system gives rise to complex queueing problems. Messages arrive from sales agents' terminals and queue up for initial identification by the control program in the central processor. Then they are placed on the appropriate transaction processing queues for subsequent treatment by the appropriate application program(s). As part of this process the application program will initiate various input/output requests for other programs or data to the many mass-storage devices on-line to the system through data channels of limited capacity. Each agent's message must compete for system resources with the many other messages which are simultaneously in the system awaiting response.

The general set of mathematical techniques which go under the general heading of 'Queueing Theory'[17] can be used to evaluate a wide variety of queueing problems. However, the characteristics of the reservations systems queues, particularly the unusual types of distribution encountered in computer systems, make an analytic solution by the classical queueing methods impracticable.

Traditionally, the solution has been sought in the construction of large, expensive computer simulation models, requiring computer power beyond the scope of Aer Lingus at the time. To overcome this limitation, some seminal work was undertaken in Aer Lingus which combined the techniques of analytic queueing theory and Monte Carlo simulation.[18]

The main parameters of interest evaluated by the models developed are the utilisation factors for the various potential bottlenecks, together with the means and variances of the message times, expressed as functions of the message rate and message mix. This type of information provides a basis on which to evaluate the conditions in terms of volume and mix of input at which system performance in terms of response time at the agents' set would degenerate below acceptable levels (such as 90 per cent of responses below 3 seconds).

While the model and approach used was not rigorous, it was tested extensively against more sophisticated computer simulation models developed by one of the major computer suppliers and found to agree with the results of this model, with a high degree of accuracy.

The original model and its derivatives have seen considerable practical application in evaluating a variety of hardware configurations for the Aer Lingus reservations system, both in its initial delivery form and subsequently.

MISCELLANEOUS

When this chapter was written (which by its nature should concentrate on the bigger accomplishments of OR in Aer Lingus), I found my mind wandering on occasion to somewhat smaller, but nonetheless pleasing pieces of OR work which stick in the memory. I would therefore like to finish this story of OR in Aer Lingus by recounting some of these.

The first is referred to in the context of 'The Total Company Model' (*above*).[9] What I find particularly attractive about this model is the ease with which the analysts were able to express the functional relationships within a complex organisation in mathematical form and their use of differential calculus to arrive at worthwhile conclusions.

In a somewhat similar vein, the second study was concerned with the problem of estimating the cost of no-shows to the airline (or more correctly the benefit of eliminating no-shows).[19] The analyst in this case was able to show that cancellations were an exponential function of time and that actual load factor on a route was logarithmically related to the break-even load factor in the steady-state condition. In fact, the actual load factor achievable on the marginal flight equals the break-even load factor.

A study into the effectiveness of the Aer Lingus sales force[20] in its allocation of call frequencies to travel agents throughout Ireland and their routing patterns, over what is arguably one of the most non-linear road systems in Europe, produced a number of very rewarding results for the analysts involved. One of the problems encountered in determining an optimal call frequency to travel agents was the task of weighing up the relative importance of such factors as annual sales on Aer Lingus services, Aer Lingus share of total business, location and stage of development (new, growing, mature). To help with the problem, the analysts were able to develop a complex series of factorial tests for the senior sales personnel in each district which produced numeric weightings for each of the relevant factors. As a result, a method of determining call frequencies, which was quantitative and intuitively acceptable to sales management, was developed. This was then used in defining the call workload.

The second pleasing outcome of this study related to the classical 'travelling salesman problem'. A deterministic simulation model was developed which routed (overnighting where necessary) salesmen throughout the relevant sales districts. To measure the mileage involved (mindful of the winding nature of the Irish road system), a five-mile square grid was developed covering the entire country using Ordnance Survey maps. The co-ordinates of each town housing a travel agent was input and a factor calculated using linear regression by which to multiply the straightline distance between any two towns. The interesting outcome was that the model was so accurate that correlation coefficients of the order of 0.97 between actual road distance travelled in a typical salesman's day and the distance computed by the model were experienced. The model did understandably make the occasional blunder, such as routing the salesman across natural boundaries such as the Shannon Estuary or large inland lakes.

Finally, I would like to mention a neat little model which was developed in the early 1970s and is still used to help with the problem of deciding the 'ideal' holding of expensive rotable/repairable units. 'Repairables' are the class of parts or assemblies which, when declared unserviceable, are routed through the appropriate repair shops, of which there are many in an aircraft maintenance environment, and eventually find their way back on the shelf in a serviceable condition.

There are a number of generalised solutions to this problem usually based on queueing theory. However, Napoli[21], at the first AGIFORS Symposium in 1961, showed using probability theory that given Poisson demand and a generalised replenishment time distribution, a stockout equation could be developed based on size of holding. This was used by United Airlines for the problem of deciding holdings of rotables at outstations.

In Aer Lingus, we were looking for a solution to the problem as it applied at the Dublin Airport maintenance base. A distinctive feature of the problem is that when a stockout occurs, or indeed when serviceable stocks run low, action takes place to expedite the affected parts currently in the repair cycle so that one or more serviceable parts are made available as quickly as possible. Thus, a part which normally had an average repair cycle time of 15 days could have this reduced to 5 days by expedite action. To reflect this, Napoli's model was extended to include an expedite feature. Firstly using Napoli's basic equation for any given part, a stock level is determined using the standard repair time for that part and the required service level (stockout reciprocal). This provides an upper limit on the desired stockholding. Two other parameters are now provided to the model, namely maximum desired level of expediting for this part number as a proportion of annual demand and average repair time under expedite action. The model then goes through a series of iterations usually resulting in a lower stock level than derived from the basic model. Also, output is the expedite stock level, that is, expedite action should be initiated when serviceable stock falls to or below this level.

CHAPTER 6

Some TCD M.Sc. Projects

ROY H W JOHNSTON

Applied Scientific Consultant

INTRODUCTION

During the period 1970-73, the author had a hand in the super-vision of seven Operations Research projects carried out by M.Sc. students at Trinity College Dublin (TCD). The projects – in several senses, experimental and innovative – commenced in 1970-71 under Professor F G Foster, head of the Department of Statistics in TCD (*see Appendix C*).

The project work constituted the practical part of the master's degree programme; there was also a lecture programme and examinations. The work was innovative in three ways. First, each project involved more than one student, usually two or three. Secondly, the terms of reference were negotiated with an outside client or sponsor, who was interested in a real solution to a real problem. And thirdly, the supervisor (ie this author) was working as consultant to the client for a fee and was responsible for the delivery of the results, irrespective of the performance of the student groups.

This procedure was possible largely because the author had opted to develop his OR consultancy as a fringe-university activity, on the grounds of his belief in the need to develop the university post-graduate system as a useful resource.

The partition of the tasks among the members of the project team was an important supervisory activity. It constituted a problem in some cases where the matching of complementary skills within the group was less than perfect. Procedures were established for setting up teams and allocating them to projects during the first term of the academic year (October to December). Dry runs on textbook case studies gave some indication of student attributes; a voting procedure was estab-lished for enabling students to express preferences for one project or another. This was taken into account when the teams were set up in December.

The projects were worked on until the following September, with bursts of initial contacting and data-gathering in the Christmas and Easter vacations, followed by full-time activity after the theoretical part of the M.Sc. course had culminated in the June examinations.

When setting up the teams, account was taken of students' primary qualifications as well as their preferences. A typical team of three would need to specialise: for example, one might concentrate on assembling and abstracting the available data into an appropriately structured (computer-accessible) database; a second might specialise in developing an appropriate decision-model capable of accessing the database for a series of 'what-if' projections; while a third, possibly playing in some ways a leading role, would determine the range of options to be tested in the light of the needs of the client. These roles however always overlapped, and in all cases it was possible to examine each student in the project as a whole, drawing out in greater detail the work for which he or she had personally been responsible.

In some cases the student report was accepted by the client; in other cases the client-report was done by the supervisor (usually when the client's deadline was inconsistent with the academic schedule). In the latter case, the student report had the status of an interesting and possibly useful background study.

The clients were in all cases either state or parastatal agencies, or agricultural co-operatives. No work was done in this mode for private industry. This perhaps reflects the dichotomy of the Irish private sector, which subdivides into (a) transnational corporations, which have their own in-house R and D facilities, usually abroad, and (b) small to medium-sized Irish-owned firms, which tend to be conservative rather than innovatory. It would appear, therefore, that there is a positive role for the state and the agricultural co-operatives in harnessing the university research system to the needs of national development.

This discussion first gives brief abstracts of all 7 projects. The first of these presents some interesting features (it is to do with the re-introduction of flax to Ireland as an economic crop) and is dealt with in some depth. The next 3 projects, all concerned with milk, are discussed in somewhat less depth and act as a basis for re-stating the problem in the contemporary environment. Extracts are given from one other project involving the analysis of a relatively complex system – the rail network. Finally, 'the transition problem' is discussed – how the momentum of projects such as these can be kept up in the aftermath, in the real world, in cases where the concept has development potential. There are unresolved problems in this area.

PROJECT ABSTRACTS

These are given in the order of their subsequent analysis: first the flax project, then the 3 projects of the 'milk group', then the 'complex system' project, and finally the school and glasshouse projects, for which (due to lack of space) the abstract must suffice.

Profitability of flax production in Ireland: The client for this study was the Bunclody Farmers' Co-operative, in collaboration with the Oakpark Centre of the Agricultural Institute.[1]

The linen industry in the north of Ireland has for some decades been dependent on imported flax, the decline in local production being attributable to problems arising in the old 'wet retting' process,[2] which was labour-intensive and polluting. Technological changes in the industry have rendered 'dew retting' acceptable,[2] so that the harvesting process now lends itself to modern agricultural mechanisation, involving investment in specialist machinery. The price is determined by quality, which depends critically on the retting process. The profitability of the overall enterprise depends on a compromise between level of mechanisation and losses due to delay in harvesting operations.

This situation was modelled by simulating the harvesting operations against a background of variable weather conditions, the latter determining both degree of retting and machine mobility. Information derived from the simulation was used to help determine the 1971 harvesting programme and in planning expansion for 1972.

Milk quality and bulk milk collection: The client here was the Lough Egish Co-operative, Co. Monaghan.[3] Bulk milk collection, with on-farm refrigeration, is the norm with the relatively large dairy-farms of Munster. In the case of the more dispersed and smaller (30 acre) farms of Monaghan, on-farm refrigeration is not always practicable (due to capital and electricity supply constraints) and the road network is relatively undeveloped. It had been decided, however, to try to implement a bulk-collection scheme despite these constraints. This had run into problems, such as queueing at the collection centre, to which various optional solutions were under consideration, for example, on-tanker refrigeration or increased central refrigeration capacity. (Pumping speed was limited by the need to refrigerate the uncooled milk loads, and this delayed tanker turnround.)

A simulation was developed to predict the overall bacterial quality of the milk in the tanker as a function of time, given the temperature and quality at successive pick-up points. The results of this contributed to the development of a procedure involving shift-work for tanker drivers, with scheduling to take account of the differing pump-off rates of refrigerated and unrefrigerated milk, collected separately. The penalty system for quality control was also tightened up. This plan was implemented and significant savings were achieved.

Milk supply seasonality in the processing industry: This and the following project were sponsored by Bord Bainne (the Irish Milk Marketing Board).[4] Both studies looked at different aspects of the same problem. The client-report was produced in this case by the author since there were data-access problems for the students; their work remains a background which had development potential had there been an immediate follow-through.

Milk processing in Ireland is dominated by the fact that the supply tends to follow the seasonal growth of the grass: a summer-winter ratio of 12:1 or even 20:1 is considered normal. As a consequence, the bulk of the production is of storable products (butter, skim powder, hard cheeses, casein), sold mostly as bulk commodities.

A techno-economic model of the industry was developed

which permitted its overall profitability to be examined in the context of an assumed reduction in seasonality ratio, (a) with the existing product mix and expanded throughput with existing capacity, and (b) with an enriched product mix (having a higher proportion of added-value products, such as would become possible with continuity of supply and improved quality and composition of milk). This expanded, deseasonalised production was compared with expanded production of the present mix, with capital investment to cope with the expanded peak capacity.

With the aid of this model, it was possible to estimate a winter premium price payable to achieve continuity of supply. The transition to the new situation, however, would be costly for the farmer (involving delaying the calving of a proportion of the herd for 6 months, with consequent loss of income) and would require positive management.

The presence of the EEC accession price bonanza militated against the recognition of the problem in 1972. It is appropriate to examine it again against the background of contemporary thinking on the CAP in the European Parliament and the existence of the 'superlevy'.

Milk seasonality and the farmer: A deterministic simulation of the national dairy herd was developed so as to enable the consequences of a variety of calving and feeding patterns to be evaluated, giving rise to various degrees of deseasonalisation of milk supply.[5] An attempt was made, using the results of research into cow physiology, to model non-linear effects in the partition of feed intake into its contribution to maintenance, weight gain, milk yield and calf weight. This was necessary because it was evident from the start that to adopt a system involving high-yielding breeds, intensively fed with concentrates (as in use to supply the urban liquid-milk market) would be an unacceptably high-cost solution. The alternative was to try to adapt a proportion of the existing herd supplying low-cost industrial milk to an autumn-calving, moderately intensive winter-feeding regime, at an acceptable additional cost.

It was concluded – taking into account seasonal effects in the beef industry (which reflected into improved prices for off-season calves and 'canners') and the extra milk yield from the extended lactation of the autumn calver on the spring grass – that deseasonalising the milk supply would, in fact, break even. The cost to the farmer would, however, be appreciable, since in the transition to autumn calving for a proportion of the herd revenue would be lost for a six-month period. This constitutes a significant barrier requiring financial incentives from the industry and/or the state if it is to be overcome.

Locomotive-linking in the national rail system: The client here was the research and planning unit of Córas Iompair Éireann, the national transport system.[6]

A simulation of all passenger and freight train movements on the national rail network was developed, such as to enable the overall locomotive requirements to be estimated for a given schedule. It proved feasible to predict locomotive needs in accordance with current experience, given the existing schedule and constraints. This suggests that the technique might be used with some confidence to predict rapidly the locomotive requirements arising from revised schedules and/ or revised constraints.

Computer-aided planning in second-level education: This project was sponsored by the Department of Education.[7] A national programme was in progress for amalgamation and integration of small schools (c 100–150 pupils) into larger units (400 pupils or more) offering a wider range of specialist subjects. An attempt was made to quantify the costs (or savings) and benefits of this process as an outline planning exercise, without attempting to get down to the level of detail required by actually doing the scheduling of the integrated system.

By combining various derived measures with appropriate weighting factors (reflecting their perceived priorities), it was possible to define a 'figure of merit' which took into account: (a) degree of satisfaction of demand for exotic subjects (such as the rarer foreign languages), (b) extent to which subjects were taught by teachers actually qualified in them, and (c) degree of teacher specialisation.

The model was partially validated with some survey data derived from a previous project which had analysed several existing schools in Galway with input to the present project in mind.

Glasshouse tomato production: An attempt was made to develop a model of a glasshouse crop production system in a specified market environment, at a level of detail which would be of use as a planning tool.[8] Particular attention was paid to winter daylight as a limiting factor.

Output from this analysis was embodied in a predictor, giving days to first harvest under standard temperature conditions as a function of planting date. This was used as input to a more general-purpose planning model which enabled various production systems (cold-house, monocrop, duocrop) to be compared in a given market background.

PROFITABILITY OF FLAX PRODUCTION

Work carried out at the Plant Sciences and Crop Husbandry Division of the Agricultural Institute at Oakpark in Carlow, between 1960 and 1967, had suggested that the growing of flax in Ireland should be competitive with France, Belgium and the Netherlands. A linen-manufacturing firm in Northern Ireland had expressed interest in establishing an alternative source of supply. Spinning tests conducted by the Linen Industry Research Institute at Lambeg, Co. Antrim, had been carried out on experimental Irish-grown dew-retted flax, giving favourable results. These had been reported in a paper to the Irish Textile Institute by Dr Michael Neenan of Oakpark in 1968, subsequently published by the Royal Irish Academy.[9]

The Bunclody Farmers' Co-op in Co. Wexford, the client for this study, had been established in 1959; by 1970, it had 150 members and a turnover of £1m. Its main business was in the sale of wheat, barley, strawberries and honey on behalf of its members. There was a need for some other crop to rotate with wheat, in the interests of disease and pest control, with a comparable financial return. The first trials of flax were made in 1966 and in June 1968 the Co-op entered into a firm contract with Kirkpatricks Ltd of Ballyclare, Co. Antrim, to harvest up to 3000 acres of flax. The 1970 planting was 610 acres. All was set for expansion of the production of an attractive crop.

In the expansion phase, it became important to plan the investment in, and operational procedures for, specialist machinery; this would be owned and managed centrally by the Co-op. It was also important to be in a position to evaluate the crop from the point of view of the farmer. To achieve these objectives, two planning models were developed – the 'farm model' and the 'machinery model'.

The farm model enabled the costs associated with the cultivation and harvesting operations, and the revenue from the sale of the crops, to be calculated for a specific farm over a number of years, taking into account crop rotation effects. It was required to work either in historic mode or as a simulation for use in forward projection. It was non-optimising: it modelled simply the consequences of the farmers' decisions regarding choice of crop and allocation of crop to specific areas of the farm. Crops catered for were grass, feeding and malting barley, oats, swedes, sugar beet, wheat and flax. There was provision for adjusting yields to respond to various rotation patterns. Thus the background of standard crops to which flax was to be compared was reasonably credible.

Flax had to be treated in more detail, with the retting process quantified. The harvesting process involved pulling the flax up by the roots (it is this that requires the relatively expensive specialist machinery) and then leaving it to lie on the ground long enough for the soil bacteria to attack the cellulose, but not for so long that the fibre is attacked; this is the so-called 'dew-retting' process.[2]

It was possible to define a 'retting index', to quantify the process and to relate it to a price, based on the tensile strength of the resulting linen. The relationship between the price and the retting index is determined by the market and was given as follows:

Retting Index:	0.1	0.2	0.3	0.4	0.5	0.6	0.7	0.8	0.9	1.0
Price:	0	0	0.68	0.8	0.91	1.0	0.92	0.86	0.79	0.73

Thus one should aim for a retting index of 0.5 to 0.7; this has to be judged by field trials and subsequently verified by laboratory testing of the fibre.

In order to predict the cumulative retting index, estimates were made of the 'rate of retting' as a function of temperature and humidity. These were derived by combining the experienced judgement of Belgian and Irish experts with weather records. The 'judgement' is summarised in the following table:

RETTING RATE ADJUSTMENT MULTIPLIER

Weather Category	Weeks for Optimal Retting	Multiplier
warm wet	3	2.00
warm dry	4-5	1.34
average	6	1.00
cold wet	7-8	0.73
cold dry	9	0.57

The 'cumulative retting index' is obtained by multiplying the 'retting rate' by the 'multiplier' in each week, depending on the weather, and summing over the weeks to date.

The weather records were taken as weekly averages for the 17 weeks of 1 July to 31 October over 11 years (ie a sunspot cycle) and were allocated to the above categories. Retting rates were established for each of the 17 weeks under average conditions; these were temperature-dependent and ranged from 0.1034 for the beginning of July to 0.0503 for the end of October. The 'cumulative retting index' was then estimated for a given weather pattern as indicated above.

This retting index predictor, using weather records from Kilkenny (the nearest available to the area under consideration), gave good agreement with actual results on a sample of farms, so that when used in simulation mode in projections it had some credibility. Thus the farm model when run gave results which took into account the price receivable for the flax resulting from a given range of harvest scheduling and weather situations.

The second planning model devised – the 'machinery model' – looked at the harvesting process from the angle of the Co-op and considered the scheduling of movements of the two types of specialist machinery around the growing region. (As well as the puller, there was a binder to lift the retted flax and bale it for transport to the central scutchingmill.) As the period between pulling and binding is needed for the retting process, the timing of these operations is of critical importance.

Farms on the model were located on a grid of 48 zones covering the whole region. A machine when finished on one farm moves to another in the nearest neighbouring zone which is known to be 'ready'. A farm has four states: not ready, ready, being worked and finished. A machine can be idle or allocated: if allocated it can be travelling or working. A machine can overnight at a farm.

The frequency distribution, mean and variance of the delays are given as output; also for each machine the total work time, travel time, revenue and cost are given (on the basis of time multiplied by unit-costs).

The simulation was run with various numbers of machines and various distributions of farms; various projection strategies were evaluated.

Subsequently, however, despite a promising start, the Bunclody initiative lapsed, due primarily to the Co-op manager falling ill at a critical period. As a consequence, owing to the uncertainty, the acreage declined and the residual farmers paid less attention to the quality of the retting process. The contract was terminated and Kirkpatricks went back, with regret, to total dependence on imported flax.[10]

MILK PROJECTS

This discussion expands on the abstracts of the 3 milk projects (*above*) and provides some additional insights into the problems as defined which were gained from the project experience. Some related unresolved problems are also specified, with suggestions as to the possible routes towards solutions.

There is a link between the 'bulk milk collection' problem and the supply seasonality problem, in that the capital invested in the system is related to its peak capacity. There is also a quality problem in the off-season, with relatively small quantities of end-lactation milk handled in a system designed for ten or twenty times the volume. Contamination is a surface phenomenon and is therefore likely to be of greater importance at low volume.

Bulk Milk Collection: In the course of the project, it emerged that the nature of the bacterial population changed when refrigeration was introduced, the 'mesophiles' being replaced by 'psychrotrophes' which are able to grow at low temperatures.[11] Growth rate/temperature curves for both classes were available for the model from laboratory studies of *E.coli* and *Pseudomonas*. There was a necessary learning process for the farmers that refrigeration was not a substitute for hygiene. This process was complicated by the fact that the traditional (and legally recognised) test for contaminated milk (methylene blue) only picks up the mesophilic bacteria. To detect the psychrotrophes, it is necessary to resort to plate-counting.

Some field tests were made to get a feel for the levels of initial contamination and the extent to which the psychrotrophes were taking over after the introduction of refrigeration. These showed up a highly variable situation which, however, improved spectacularly during the course of the project (an example of the 'Heisenberg Effect'[12]). Word got around that something was afoot and farmers started paying attention to cleaning their vessels. Plate-counting, which had not yet become the practice at the Co-op quality control lab, was sub-contracted in from the Regional Technical College in Dundalk.

The problem of electricity-loading was at that time being approached by the ESB, who were encouraging the 'ice-bank' principle to spread the load over the whole day using a low-power heat-pump. This equipment, however, was relatively expensive and the Monaghan farmers preferred to invest in small mobile systems with relatively high power consumption over a short cooling time. When all worked together at milking-time, an unacceptably high load was placed on the extended rural electricity distribution network. Thus the ESB was then, and still remains, concerned about the situation; electronic load management systems have subsequently been introduced for use at farm level. In some cases, standby generators have been installed, so that milking machines can be operated even if there is a power-cut. In such cases, it sometimes turns out that it pays to use the standby generator to carry the peak load, rather than to pay to have the distribution network upgraded.

This suggests the need for some in-depth analysis of the rural energy economy: for example, the possibility of using the heat of the cows' milk, pumped up to an appropriate temperature, as the main energy source for the domestic and farm hot-water supply; also the possibility of using the standby (or 'peak-chopper') generator engine as a 'combined heat and power' (CHP) source. The matching of this concept to the market needs and the technological possibilities is an opportunity on the borderline of OR and systems engineering.

Seasonality and the Processing Industry: We are here in the presence of the Frankenstein monster created by the Common Agricultural Policy (CAP). When this OR project was undertaken in 1972, Ireland had just become a member of the EEC and was in the grip of the euphoria generated by the new milk price regime. Money could be made simply with more of the same; adapting the product mix to market need was low on the agenda. Butter, powdered skim, bulk commodity hard cheese and casein were the principal products. There was no price differential in favour of commodity cheese; if there had been, then 'extending the cheese season' would have helped to make the case for deseasonalising the supply. (Cheese can only be produced with quality mid-lactation milk.) If anything, EEC price policy favoured butter and powdered skim at the expense of cheese, thus keeping the Irish milk processing industry in a 'bulk commodity disposal operation' trap and discouraging creative marketing.

The problem, however, has at last begun to be recognised in the presence of the 'superlevy' and the threat of drastic CAP reform. Public opinion will no longer tolerate mountains of unwanted butter, powdered skim or beef. There is scope for another hard look at the industry, its product mix and its approach to the market. The only possible future is to get out of bulk commodity products 'produced for intervention' and go for up-market value-added products. Lack of continuity of supply is the principal obstacle to this transition.

Some tentative steps have been taken by a few small local quality cheese enterprises and by the yoghurt producers. This type of activity needs enhancement. The planning of the transition is a challenge to be faced at government level: can we create an aggressive up-market quality food industry, and get our farmers to supply it reliably?

Incidentally, most calves are born in spring, so that the beef industry faces the same seasonality problems. Any new analysis of the problem, based on the techno-economic modelling of the linked agricultural and industrial systems, must look into both beef and milk as two related sub-systems, with a common interest in the shared problem of continuity of supply.

Seasonality and the Farmer: The principal barrier to the farmer making the transition to a deseasonalised milk supply pattern is the lag in revenue resulting from delaying the calving of some of the herd until autumn. This assumes importance in proportion as the farmer's income is dependent on volume of production.

The current EEC policy of subsidising agriculture at the expense of the consumer with a dear food policy has two main pathological effects: (a) supply is unmatched to demand and 'mountains' are generated, and (b) intensive production is encouraged, with maximal use of pesticides, antibiotics and veterinary products, which are needed to keep animals alive under high-stress conditions. (Abuse of antibiotics is on the way to becoming a public health problem, as resistant strains of pathogens build up.)

An alternative policy is feasible, whereby instead of the consumer subsidising agriculture on a volume basis, the taxpayer subsidises the family farm by paying a social wage to the farmer, who would be contracted to manage the rural environment in the public interest. Any farming activity carried out as a component of the overall rural environment management (the latter could include care of wildlife habitats, maintenance of footpaths and ramblers' rights of way) would be subject to market prices and would gain the farmer an additional economic income over and above the social wage. Intensive practices leading to mountains of unwanted produce would be replaced by traditional biological agriculture, with good soil management and crop rotations, as outlined in a recent EEC Parliamentary Report.[13]

In the context of a revised CAP, the cost of transition for a proportion of the herd to autumn-calving would be reduced in proportion as the social wage assumed a greater relative importance in the farm income. The consequences of CAP reform constitute a fruitful field for the systems modeller.[14]

THE IRISH RAIL NETWORK

The rail system simulation took as its point of departure the existing manual procedures by skilled schedulers having a detailed knowledge of the railway system. The following extracts from the report give some impression of the simulation. The report was handed over as a going concern for further development by CIE research staff.

'. . . A timetable of train movements is first established, to cater for a given regular demand for passenger and freight services. This must be so arranged that free paths and platform facilities are available at appropriate times. . . a locomotive is then assigned to each train. . . two to the heavier trains (double heading). It is desirable that each locomotive should be assigned to a circular series of trains over a period of not more than 3 days. . . and that the locomotive then returns to the first train in the series. This series of journeys is known as a 'link'. Allowance must be made in the links for routine maintenance. . . decoupling and shunting time must also be allowed for. . .

'. . . In establishing the links. . . the timetable may be adjusted slightly . . . provided a free path is available. The number of links is the number of locomotives required to run the system. . . . Setting up a complete new link system takes about three man-months. . . the system cannot be adapted quickly to changes in policy or demand. . .

'The model works as far as possible in the same way as the manual system. . . . The information in the daily train timetable is sorted into a list of arrivals and departures ('events'). . . relevant information about events is stored. . . . For each station in interest, a sub-list of events is set up. . . . Stations of interest include terminals. . . . Stations where fuel or maintenance facilities are available, and major junctions, are known as 'centres'. A train which stops at an intermediate centre for long enough to allow fuel service or change of locomotive is split into sub-trains or 'segments'. . .

'A list of the stock of locomotives at each centre at midnight on Sunday, and of those still running, is fed into the model. The program then works through the master-list of events . . . allocating suitable locomotives to departures and relegating locomotives to stock on arrival. . . . Choice of locomotive . . . is made according to specified rules. . . . if none is available, then various actions can be taken. . .

'The main piece of essential input data is the train timetable. When transformed and coded, it consists of about 1200 events; 16 items of data were needed on each event; 100 centres were considered, at any given centre up to 200 events might occur. . . .

'Preliminary runs showed that a large saving in locomotives could be made by allowing light-engine runs within the Dublin Complex. A special queue was therefore set up. . . . and the event-selection routine modified to regard all Dublin events as occurring at one centre. . . .'

THE TRANSITION PROBLEM

It is necessary to conclude by reminding the reader that the above systems modelling was done in high-level language (Fortran or PL1) on a university mainframe computer. In most, if not all, cases it could now be done without difficulty on a personal microcomputer.

In no case was the software 'engineered', that is, it was understood by the person or people who had produced it, but was not readily transportable. While to some extent the programs were 'structured', they would not have been done rigorously according to the rules of 'structured programming'.

Thus if any of the models were to become anything more than supports for a one-off study (for which purpose they were of course useful, indeed indispensable), they would need to be taken into the clients' systems along with their producers for a period of in-house development or for a protracted period of further problem analysis using the skills developed during the project.

Alternatively (and this would tend to be the modern solution), they would need to be processed by a specialist software engineering group into transportable marketable packages.

In the 1972 environment, it proved possible in some cases for the students on completion of their projects to be recruited on a temporary basis for some follow-through work. This constituted good experience and in several cases it led to long-term jobs in the general area of the project (though in no case with the original client).

In the case of one project (the school model) an attempt was made subsequently to 'software engineer' it, with the aid of a computer science graduate (who had not been exposed to the problem). This was not successful, as the emphasis in the software engineering was on 'data-processing efficiency', as in payroll packages, rather than on making it friendly and accessible to a long-term user who was problem- (rather than technique-) orientated. The 'culture gap' between OR and computer people was recognised as a result of this episode; it remains a problem to this day.

If the full potential of modern microcomputer technology is to be taken up, it is going to be necessary for OR people to get to interact with specialist developers of reliable portable software, producing marketable problem-solving packages for market niches identifed by OR consultants. Alternatively OR practitioners are going to have to become their own software engineers, making use of advanced development packages where necessary.

CHAPTER 7

Operations Research and Energy

RICHARD KAVANAGH

Bord Na Móna

HISTORICAL PERSPECTIVE

The use of analytical techniques in energy matters in Ireland dates from the late 1960s when J L Booth, at the Economic and Social Research Institute, published a series of studies on energy forecasts based on econometric forecasting models.[1]

Following this publication no further activities were undertaken until 1970 when the Fletcher Report on the ESB was published.[2] This report contained electricity forecasts which were focused primarily on trend growth rates derived from historical trend data. In 1974 Bunyan published the results of a M.Sc. Thesis completed in 1972, which contained energy demand forecasts based on Booth's econometric models using more up-to-date information.[3]

The 1970s represented a watershed in energy matters. The oil supply crisis of 1973-74, compounded by the effects of the supply disruption in 1979-80, delivered shocks to the world economy (and to Ireland in particular, where the effects last to this day) despite the recent decline of crude oil prices to 1973-74 levels.

In the aftermath of the 1973-74 crisis, energy matters assumed a very high profile at political and macro-economic levels, which was reflected in a heightened interest in energy analysis. This review describes these developments.

THE OFFICIAL RESPONSE

The major difficulty bedevilling energy analysts in the 1960s and the early '70s, and which became much more severe in the post-1973-74 climate of urgency, was the lack of adequate and accurate statistical data, particularly at sectoral (residential, industrial, commercial and transport) levels. These were required as a basis for further analysis and forecasting, leading to the formation of energy policies by the government.

The Department of Transport and Power (currently the Department of Energy) responded to the difficulties in three ways – by upgrading its statistics activities, by calling upon the assistance of the Operations Research (OR) Section of the Department of the Public Service (DPS) and by commissioning a report on energy matters from E Henry of the Economic and Social Research Institute.

The interim report of the DPS Group (compiled by J Cantwell and B Lenehan) was ready by December 1975[4] and focused on two main areas of interest: forecasts of primary energy demand and a national energy model.

The DPS forecasting model: Essentially the DPS forecasting model consisted of a relationship between the growth rates in GNP and in energy consumption. Thus:

$$G R = 3.446 \exp (-0.7x)$$

where: G R = growth ratio, ie ratio of percentage increase in energy consumption to percentage increase in GNP;

x = per capita GNP in 1963 US dollars;

$r^2 = 0.94$

The model was developed from historical data for seven European countries using regression techniques. Projections of demand up to 1981, given different GNP growth assumptions, were developed using this model, from a 1974 base. (The results of these and other forecasting models are compared below.)

The DPS national energy model: The simplified national energy model developed by the DPS group involved for the first time in Ireland the application of linear programming techniques to a flow diagram of the energy system (*see Fig. 1*).

For illustrative purposes, the objective funtion chosen was to minimise conversion losses subject to certain capacity and production constraints. The results indicated how losses could be minimised (eg by minimal utilisation of electricity for heating purposes). It should be noted that final demand is defined as the output of the secondary fuel sector and therefore takes

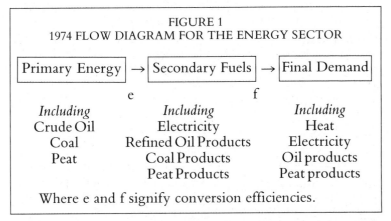

FIGURE 1
1974 FLOW DIAGRAM FOR THE ENERGY SECTOR

| Primary Energy | → | Secondary Fuels | → | Final Demand |
| e | | | f | |

Including	*Including*	*Including*
Crude Oil	Electricity	Heat
Coal	Refined Oil Products	Electricity
Peat	Coal Products	Oil products
	Peat Products	Peat products

Where e and f signify conversion efficiencies.

account of conversion losses from the primary fuel (eg crude oil to refined diesel oil, or peat to electricity).

The DPS Group was expanded in 1974 to include the author and later M Rooney. Due to the considerable efforts being devoted at the time and in later years to improving the statistical database and to developing forecasts for the Department of Transport and Power, together with a lack of resources, the development of the linear programming model was discontinued.

The Henry Report: The Henry Report[5] was published in 1976 and addressed the conservation potential and options for Ireland for the period 1975-85. The report represented a further significant advance in analysing the energy sector. The forecasting section of the report relied on the DPS forecasting model in developing projections to the year 1985.

The Government discussion document: Following the various efforts in database improvement, forecasting and policy analysis, the energy discussion document *Energy-Ireland* was published by the Government in 1978.[6] The forecasting section of the report, prepared by the DPS Group and using the DPS forecasting model further refined on a sectoral basis, contained demand projections up to 1990.

THE NATIONAL SCIENCE COUNCIL / NATIONAL BOARD FOR SCIENCE AND TECHNOLOGY (NBST)

A simulation model: In parallel with the work of the DPS Group, the National Science Council (later reconstituted as the National Board for Science and Technology/NBST) initiated a project on energy analysis based on participation in an international co-operative agreement between the International Energy Agency (IEA) countries. The project focused initially on the development of a detailed database on energy flows in the Irish economy. This was a considerable task since it involved collecting detailed data at a disaggregated level not only on primary energy flows but also on final and useful energy flows – a task never before undertaken. The reference year chosen was 1974 and the data were fed into a large simulation model.[7] Projections of useful energy demand (eg residential heat, electricity) were prepared for each disaggregated demand sector (eg central heating, electricty for cooking) and fed into the simulation model to examine the impact on primary and secondary energy and on inter-fuel substitution, while also allowing for the penetration of new technologies, such as natural gas for central heating.

This work represented a major step forward in three respects, namely the development of a detailed disaggregated simulation model of the energy system, the development of a detailed database for the model and the use of useful energy demand rather than primary energy demand projections. Thus the referred model was similar to the DPS model with the added refinement of a useful energy demand module where final energy is converted (eg by an open fire or cooker) to useful energy (heat).

In addition, the concept of international co-operation in the area of energy analysis enabled Ireland, a small economy with limited expertise in the area, to gain access and make significant contributions to the development of the sophisticated models then being developed at the large research institutes in Germany (Kernforschungsanlage / KFA in Julich) and the United States (Brookhaven National Laboratory in New York State). Also, it enabled active participation from two of Ireland's energy utilities: the Electricity Supply Board and Bord Gais Éireann.

The Markal linear programming model: Work on the energy model was continued in the late 1970s by the author and J Brady. The model was transformed from a simulation exercise into a full-scale linear programming time-stepped model through the work of the IEA groups in Germany and the USA. The results of the NBST group were published in 1980.[8]

The model (referred to as Markal, for Market Allocation) was operated by feeding a projected useful energy demand profile into a linear programming matrix representing a series of fuel and technology options, while allowing for movements in energy prices, structural changes in demand, various supply constraints, inter-fuel and inter-technology competition and substitution, energy conservation and numerous new technologies (eg heat pumps, district heating, wind energy). The model was thus demand-driven and was optimised at 5-year intervals within an overall 30-year period. A variety of objective functions, such as minimum cost and minimum oil consumption, was used in the analysis. Comprehensive descriptions of the Markal model were published in 1979[9] and 1981.[10]

The work on Markal continued into the early 1980s and J Brady published an up-dated version of energy supply and demand in 1983.[11] This work has since been discontinued.

Demand forecasting models: The NBST group prepared a series of useful energy demand projections for use in conjunction with the Markal model. The methodology consisted of a bottom-up, rather than a top-down, approach. Each sector of the energy economy was broken down in great detail in terms of useful energy demand. Future demand was calculated on the basis of detailed sectoral data (eg industrial start-ups, housing completion statistics, projections of population growth and family composition, number and mix of devices such as cookers, refrigerators, central heating units, etc). These were aggregated to give total useful energy demand. By feeding the demand profile into the Markal model and having chosen an appropriate objective function the primary energy required to meet the useful energy demand emerged from the analysis.

Separately, the NBST group, expanded to include L Killen,

also prepared and published primary energy demand projections.[12, 13, 14] These were based on econometric models and contained for the first time an analytical approach to the estimation of the conservation effects which came about in previous years because of price and GNP effects.

THE ECONOMIC AND SOCIAL RESEARCH INSTITUTE (ESRI)

The Henry Report (*above*) was carried out for the Department of Transport and Power and published in 1976.[5] Subsequently, in 1979, Henry published the results of research into the use of input-output models of the Irish economy as a basis for energy forecasting, in particular for electricity forecasting.[15]

In the same year a joint ESRI/NBST publication[16] sought to bring together the results of the two approaches (linear programming and generalised economic models) to energy analysis. Using a convergence loop it was possible to reconcile the two approaches, but nevertheless the study highlighted the differences between them and great attention had to be directed at the detailed assumptions in both cases to ensure that major convergence occurred.

In 1980 S Scott of ESRI published a series of econometric-based forecasts of primary energy demand.[17]

COMMISSION OF THE EUROPEAN COMMUNITIES (CEC)

During the 1970s, the CEC initiated a community-wide effort on energy analysis through its first and second energy research and development programmes. Ireland participated in this programme through the NBST (R Kavanagh and L Killen) and ESRI (E Henry). Later, as the work progressed, the Irish responsibility was taken on by the Software Engineering Laboratory of the Computer Science Department at Trinity College Dublin (K Ryan).

Essentially the project consisted of three separate models:

MEDEE-3:   a detailed techno-economic model which was used to forecast final energy demand;

EFOM-12-C: a linear programming model which generated the optimal primary energy supply
to meet a given final energy demand;[18]

EURECA: a model which reconciled the macro-
economic variables (prepared from the
CEC macroeconomic model COMET
IV) with energy price and supply variables.

Case studies were prepared for each member country and aggregated to provide an overview for the entire Community. The results of the most recent analysis were published in 1986.[19]

COMPARISON OF FORECASTING MODELS

The validity of any forecasting model can be measured only by comparing its performance with the actual out-turns. Table 1 contains the various primary energy projections made by the different energy groups from Booth's 1966-67 forecasts[1] to the more recent ones of Killen[14] and the CEC.[19]

In terms of convergence with actual primary energy demand over the period, a number of features emerge:

(1) both the DPS (1975) and the Henry (1976) projections were consistently better than any of the other projections;

(2) both sets of projections are based on the growth ratio concept;

(3) in the short-term the econometric models developed by Kavanagh and Killen performed well;

(4) in all cases the major impact on performance was determined by the accuracy of GNP forecasts. In the case of the DPS Group they successfully predicted a low-GNP growth scenario over the period to 1981. In Henry's case the high growth scenario of the late 1970s, combined with a low-growth scenario for the 1980s, provided an accurate estimation of demand. For Kavanagh and Killen the models were successful in that fairly accurate assessments of short-run GNP growth were available.

The conclusions of the comparison would appear to be that the growth ratio model is good for both short- and long-term

TABLE 1

COMPARISON OF FORECAST AND ACTUAL PRIMARY ENERGY DEMAND (MTOE)* : 1970–1985

Forecast** and Ref.	Year	1970	1976	1977	1978	1979	1980	1981	1982	1983	1984	1985
Booth[1]	1966,1967	*5.8*										
Bunyan[3]	1974						17.0					
DPS[4]	1975						8.2	8.5				
							8.8	9.2				
							9.4	9.9				
							10.1	10.7				
Henry[5]	1976		7.1	7.1	7.2	7.3	7.4	7.6	7.7	7.8	7.9	8.0
			7.1	7.2	7.4	7.8	8.1	8.7	8.8	9.2	9.6	9.9
			7.1	7.3	7.9	8.5	9.1	9.7	10.3	10.9	11.6	12.2
Geraghty[7]	1977											13.7
Government[6]	1978											13.2
Henry[15]	1979						9.0					11.3
							9.6					12.8
							9.9					14.7
Brady/Kavanagh[8]	1980											10.1
Kavanagh/Killen[12,13]	1980						8.3					9.2
							8.4					9.8
							8.5					10.5
							8.6					11.1
Killen[14]	1981											10.4
												9.8
												9.6
												9.0
CEC[19]	1986											9.0
												10.4
												9.8
												9.6
												9.0
Actual Demand		5.8	7.0	7.4	7.7	8.6	8.3	8.2	8.2	8.2	8.1	8.4

* Million tonnes of oil equivalent.   ** Multiple entries correspond to different scenarios.   Entries in *italics* are close to actual demand.

projections of energy demand; that econometric models can be useful for short-run demand; that accurate GNP projections are required; and that a number of growth scenarios should be chosen to encompass the likely range of GNP growth and energy demand.

ENERGY MODELS

In view of the discussion so far on energy forecasting models, the main prerequisite to the successful exploitation of detailed techno-economic models is a set of realistic demand forecast scenarios which are in turn based on realistic GNP growth assumptions. If these are available, then techno-economic models are of value in assessing the interplay of various fuels and technologies, inter-fuel substitution and structural changes. Such models can provide an understanding of the complexities of the energy system. They can also be useful in examining the sensitivity and robustness of the energy system to different growth scenarios and to the impact of various abrupt changes, such as an oil or gas find or further oil supply disruption.

ENERGY-PRODUCTION MODELLING

Efforts in the application of OR and management sciences techniques to the production side of energy have been fairly limited to date, with the exception of the NBST work on Markal which involved energy supply, production and conversion modules (*above*). The Electricity Supply Board and the Irish Gas Board were both involved in this work and, insofar as is known, there has been little follow-on activity. In more recent times, Bord na Móna has initiated the development of a detailed production-transport-conversion model using simulation and mathematical techniques.[20]

CONCLUDING REMARKS

Over the period from the mid-1970s, immediately after the first oil-supply crisis, to the early 1980s significant efforts were made by a number of groups in the public service to grapple with the problems of energy forecasting and analysis. Since the early 1980s, the emphasis on energy matters has declined significantly world-wide and this has been reflected in Ireland also, where activity in general macro-modelling and forecasting is currently at a very low level. Virtually all of the groups engaged in the work discussed here have now disbanded and one might ask if the lack of continuity of effort may generate future difficulties. It could be argued that it would be advisable to have one small group engaged in such work on a continual basis.

CHAPTER 8

Simulation and its applications

FRANCIS NEELAMKAVIL

Trinity College Dublin

WHAT IS SIMULATION?

A system is a collection of interacting elements or components that act together to achieve a common goal. A model is a simplified representation of a system. And simulation is the process of imitating the important features of the system by building and experimenting with the model of the system.

A model adapted for simulation on a computer is known as a computer simulation model, or simply simulation model. Simulation is not a fully developed science. Human judgement, experience and intuition do play an important role in the practice of simulation. Simulation helps us to evaluate alternative solutions to a given problem quickly, cheaply and harmlessly without conducting live experiments. Management games for training managers, graphical illustration of the effects of wearing seat belts in a motor crash and the study of the behaviour of a nuclear reactor under adverse conditions are examples of simulation models in action. Application areas of simulation include agriculture, aircraft industries, biology, business, medicine, computer science, hospital administration, finance, manufacturing, chemical industries, oil exploration, resource allocation, robotics and VLSI design.

There are two basic approaches to simulation, namely continuous and discrete. In a continuous approach, we use a continuous model of the system where the variables undergo smooth changes (eg current, voltage) in their values. In the discrete approach, we use a discrete model and here the variables change in discrete steps (eg number of customers in a bank). Simulation of continuous systems involves the generation of numerical solutions satisfying the mathematical equations which describe the model for a given set of initial conditions. Continuous system models are generally described by differential and sometimes algebraic equations. Discrete system simulation consists of the collection and analysis of data obtained by generating events at different points in time in a computer model of the system.

A clock (digital counter) is set at the centre of every simulation program and by scaling the time unit in the simulation model, one can simulate the system in real time, compressed time or expanded time. The following algorithm illustrates the basic principle behind the execution of a simple discrete system simulation program.

STEP 1

Create simulation model
Initialise simulation clock

STEP 2

Find next potential event
Advance clock to next event time
Change system state
Collect statistics
If simulation termination condition is not satisfied, go to Step 2.

STEP 3

Generate statistics
STOP

Simulation of systems need not always involve the use of computers. However, nowadays computers are so handy that almost all simulations are done on computers. This discussion will be confined to the simulation of systems on digital computers, even though analogue and hybrid computers are still being used for special applications. For a detailed discussion of various topics on simulation, the reader is referred to Gordon (1978)[1] and Neelamkavil (1986).[2]

PROBLEM-SOLVING BY SIMULATION

Problem-solving by simulation is an iterative process. The major steps in systems simulation are (1) systems analysis; (2) definition of hypothesis; (3) formulation of models; (4) simplification and validation of models; (5) identification of simulation strategy; (6) computer implementation of the simulation model; and (7) collection, analysis and interpretation of simulation results.

Several simulation runs and subsequent analysis and interpretation of results may be necessary to obtain a satisfactory solution to a given problem. The experimental nature of simulation should not be underestimated and a good knowledge of 'experimental design' is a highly desirable quality of a good simulation analyst.

Another feature of simulation is that it is an experimental problem-solving technique and is expensive in terms of manpower and computer time. Simulation is sometimes referred to as a method of last resort. This method of problem-solving becomes attractive only when the given problem cannot be solved by conventional analytic, numeric or experimental methods within a reasonable time and at a reasonable cost and risk. For example, simulation becomes more attractive in the study of the performance of an oil-rig, the behaviour of a space vehicle, the design of a new computer or the feasibility of a proposed manufacturing system. Simulation results are likely to be less accurate than analytic solutions and the main objective of simulation is to find satisfactory solutions to practical problems.

IMPORTANCE OF MODELS

A model is a simplified representation of a system and simulation is the process of mimicking the behaviour of the system with the help of a computerised model. Obviously, the computer model must be an adequate representation of the real system and capable of generating all important events that occur during the normal operation of the system. There are different types of models. Mental models (eg how to make a cup of coffee) exist only in our minds; physical models (eg model of a house or car) are made of tangible elements. Mathematical equations, logical relations, graphs, pictures and so on form another type of model, known as symbolic models. For example, a discrete model used for simulating a small bank with one teller includes a simulation clock (counter), a description of logical sequence of events and operations, priority rules, methods for computing interarrival and service time of customers and procedures for collecting statistics.

Similarly, a continuous model used for simulating a simple car-suspension system can be described by:

$$M\ddot{x} + D\dot{x} + Kx = F(t)$$

where $M\ddot{x}$ = reactive force due to mass M of the car
$= M\,d^2x/dt^2$;

$D\dot{x}$ = reactive force due to the damping factor D of the dashpot = $D\,dx/dt$;

Kx = reactive force due to the stiffness K of the spring;

$F(t)$ = applied external force;

x = displacement of the system at time t.

Models are used to improve understanding of the system and also to predict and control the behaviour of the system. Symbolic models, and in particular mathematical models, play an important role in systems simulation. A theory expressed in mathematical form is a mathematical model. The dynamic mathematical models are expressed in terms of differential equations, while static mathematical models are represented by algebraic equations. Some mathematical models are not amenable to analytic solutions and numerical approximation techniques may be necessary to extract usable solutions. The dynamic, numeric, mathematical models form the core of simulation models. However, it must be emphasised that a simulation model need not necessarily be mathematical in character; a set of logical relations could be adequate in some cases.

By now, it should be clear that simulation cannot proceed without a good model and hence the importance of modelling in simulation. Modelling is the process of establishing relationships between different elements in the system and an informal modelling methodology has emerged over the last few years. First, there must be a clear statement of the problem and this is followed by systems analysis, hypothesis testing, formulation of a general model and derivation of a simplified, specific computable model. A model must be verified (checking model implementation with design specification) and validated (ie prove that the model is an acceptable representation of the real system) before it can be used for practical simulation. Strictly speaking, a model cannot be validated. However, in practice, a collection of theoretical, heuristic and experimental methods as well as experience and judgement are helpful in model validation. Validation of models by statistical hypothesis testing can lead to two types of errors – type 1 error (model builder's risk) and type 2 error (model user's risk). Accepting the validity of the model when it is actually invalid results in type 2 error; rejecting the validity of the model when it is actually valid leads to type 1 error. Close co-operation and compromise between model-sponsors, model-builders and model-users will be absolutely essential for successful completion of any major simulation modelling exercise.

MODELLING AND SIMULATION – A SIMPLE EXAMPLE

Consider the modelling and simulation of a surgery with N doctors. The main purpose of this study is to examine the average waiting time of patients, average number of patients waiting and the average busy period of the doctors during a typical working day. The information gained by simulating this and other surgery configurations (eg effect of the number of doctors on patient waiting time, number of patients waiting and the cost of running the surgery) will be useful not only for future planning, but also for improving the overall efficiency of the surgery.

For simplicity, let us consider the situation where N=1 and FIFO (first-in, first-out) principle is followed in servicing the patients. In other words, we have converted our surgery system into a simple single-channel, single-server queueing system. The extension of the modelling and simulation strategy to multi-channel, multi-server queueing models is reasonably straightforward.

The first step in modelling our surgery system is to identify the logical sequences of events and operations, and to estimate the time required for various operations. This can be done by observing the existing system; if the system is not observable (system may not exist), the necessary data can be derived by examining the properties of a single-channel, single-server queueing system. The collection, analysis and reduction of data may require a good knowledge of statistics. Arrival and departure of patients are the two basic events which bring about changes in system variables and the interarrival time and service time of patients are the two statistics required for modelling the system. Analytical functions can be used to generate interarrival time and service time, if it is possible to show that the interarrival time and service time do have standard statistical distributions. For example, negative exponentially distributed event times can be generated from cumulative distribution functions with the help of random numbers which are uniformly distributed in the range 0 to 1. If it is not possible to fit a well-known distribution to observed data, then the interarrival times and service times are generated empirically by using interpolation techniques.

All the necessary elements for modelling are now ready and the next step is to write a computer program which generates the sequence of events in the correct order and at the appropriate time. Provision is also made for the collection of necessary statistics, which are printed out at the end of the simulation run. The patients' arrival rate and service rate (or the empirical distribution) are the inputs and the utilisation of doctor, average number of patients waiting, average waiting time and the average time spent in the surgery are the outputs. The basic algorithm for the simulation of the surgery is shown below, where the interarrival time and the service time are generated from appropriate distributions by separate procedures and the simulation clock is basically a digital counter.

STEP 1

Create model

Generate INTERARRIVAL TIME of patients

Set NEXT ARRIVAL TIME to INTERARRIVAL TIME

Set NEXT DEPARTURE TIME equal to infinity.

STEP 2

If next event is an arrival, go to Step 5

Update simulation clock to NEXT DEPARTURE TIME

Collect statistics

Increase the NO. OF PATIENTS SERVICED by one

Decrease the NO. OF PATIENTS IN SURGERY by one

If no more patients in surgery, go to Step 3
Generate SERVICE TIME and compute NEXT DEPARTURE TIME
Collect statistics
Go to Step 4

STEP 3

Set NEXT DEPARTURE TIME equal to infinity

STEP 4

If simulation STOP condition is not satisfied, go to Step 2
Print statistics
STOP

STEP 5

Update simulation clock to NEXT ARRIVAL TIME
Collect statistics
Increase the NO. OF PATIENTS ARRIVED by one
Increase the NO. OF PATIENTS IN SURGERY by one
Generate INTERARRIVAL TIME and compute NEXT ARRIVAL TIME
If NO. OF PATIENTS IN SURGERY is greater than one, go to Step 6
Start service for the patient just arrived
Generate SERVICE TIME and compute NEXT DEPARTURE TIME
Collect statistics
Go to Step 4

STEP 6

The patient who just arrived waits in surgery
Go to Step 4
END

The Pascal implementation of the above algorithm produced the following results:

INPUT:

Arrival rate: 0.22/minute ⎫ Negative exponentially
Service rate: 0.36/minute ⎭ distributed

OUTPUT
Average waiting time of patient: 0.06 minutes
Average number of patients waiting: 0.79
Average busy period of the doctor: 60.3%

It is important to observe that the above algorithm is very general in nature and can be adapted to simulate a variety of other systems, such as banks, restaurants, airports, supermarkets, production lines or machine shops. The vast majority of discrete systems are stochastic in character and random number generators (*below*) are required in the simulation of such systems. Simulation experiments are repeated several times with different sets of random numbers and the results are subjected to statistical analysis before they are used for practical applications.

ROLE OF RANDOM NUMBERS

No paper on simulation would be complete without an introduction to random number generators, which are an integral part of every discrete system simulation package. The quality of the random numbers used in a simulation will have a major impact on the reliability and the usefulness of the simulation results. The methods for the generation and testing of random numbers are examined here, and then followed by a discussion on how random numbers are used in simulation.

If a variable x can take any value in a given range with equal probability and the future values of x are not influenced by its past values, then x is said to be a random variable. Random numbers are essentially independent random variables uniformly distributed in the range 0 to 1. The concept of random sampling to estimate statistical distribution functions was introduced by W E Gossett in 1908, writing under the pseudonym of 'Student' from Guinness' Brewery in Dublin.[3] This was the beginning of the systematic study of random processes.

Random numbers can be generated in many ways. True random numbers can be generated only by physical methods. The computer-generated random numbers, using some recursive algorithms, are reproducible and hence known as pseudorandom numbers. Physical methods for random number generation include flipping coins, rolling dice, shuffling cards, the use of roulette wheels, electronic randomisers and radioactive sources. Currently, the most widely used method of generating pseudo-random numbers (or random numbers, for short) is the congruential methods invented by Lehmer in 1951.[4] The general algorithm for producing the random sequence is:

$$x_{i+1} = a\, x_i + c \pmod{m}$$
$$= \text{remainder of } [(\,a\, x_i + c)\, /\, m]$$

where a, c, m = constants

x_i = sequence of random numbers

x_o = initial value of x_i, called the Seed

When c>0, the method is known as Mixed Congruential method; when c=0, it is called the Multiplicative Congruential method. The random numbers in the range 0 to 1 can be produced from:

$$x_{i+1} = a\, x_i + c \pmod{m}$$
$$r_i = (x_i\, /m) < 1;\ i = 0.1 \ldots$$

The selection of the constants a, m and x_o is critical for ensuring the quality of the generator.[5, 6]

A random number generator is said to be good if it is portable and the output sequence is uniformly distributed, statistically independent, reproducible and non-repeating for any desired lengths. There are several procedures including the Frequency test, Serial test, Runs test and Gap test for testing random numbers. A detailed discussion on the generation and testing of random numbers can be found in Knuth.[6]

If a pseudo-random number Y is used to generate another variable X, then X is called a random variate. The random variates required in simulation experiments are generated by transforming a sequence of random numbers uniformly distributed in the range 0 to 1 into samples from appropriate probability distributions. The Inverse Transformation and Rejection methods are two of the most commonly used methods for generating random variates. The interarrival time and service time are computed several times during the simulation of our doctor's surgery discussed above. The exponentially distributed event time t can be generated from:

$$t = (-\text{mean})\log(r)$$

where mean = mean of the exponential distribution
r = uniformly distributed random number
in the range 0 to 1

The random variates can also be generated empirically from a finite number of data points using interpolation techniques.

The generation of discrete random variates from an empirical distribution can be illustrated by the following example. Suppose there are three checkouts in a supermarket and it was observed that, on average, half of the customers used checkout 1, a quarter used checkout 2 and the remaining customers used checkout 3. We want to outline a procedure for assigning appropriate checkouts (random variate) to customers in a simulation model of the supermarket. We have:

j	1	2	3
p(j)	1/2	1/4	1/4
F(j)	1/2	3/4	1

where $p(j)$ = discrete probability distribution
$F(j)$ = cumulative distribution function

The following procedure accomplishes the desired random assignment of checkouts to various customers:

If $0 \leq r < \frac{1}{2}$, assign Checkout 1 to current customer;
If $\frac{1}{2} \leq r < \frac{3}{4}$, assign Checkout 2 to current customer;
If $\frac{3}{4} \leq r < 1$, assign Checkout 3 to current customer;
where r = a uniformly distributed random number in the range 0 to 1.

COMPUTER SIMULATION LANGUAGES

Systems simulation can be carried out in a variety of computer languages. Simulation programs have been written in Fortran, Pascal, PL/1, Basic, Ada, etc. However, simulation programming is made easier, cheaper and faster by using special-purpose simulation languages. In general, programming in general-purpose languages is more difficult, but the resulting programs are more efficient in terms of flexibility and speed of execution. GASP, GPSS, SIMSCRIPT, SLAM and

SIMULA are some of the popular discrete system simulation languages; ACSL, CSMP, CSSL and DYNAMO are widely used for the simulation of continuous systems.[2] A catalogue of micro, mini and mainframe simulation software can be found in SCS.[7]

A good simulation language must have facilities for:
  (a) easy installation, use and maintenance;
  (b) modelling the system fairly easily;
  (c) creation and deletion of events with ease;
  (d) good database management;
  (e) quick detection and correction of errors;
  (f) generation of a variety of random variates;
  (g) interactive graphical simulation;
  (h) efficient collection, analysis and display of results;
  (i) user friendly input/output;
  (j) self-documentation.

The availability of cheap machines and user-friendly simulation languages have popularised the usage of simulation for problem-solving in a wide variety of disciplines. Several simulation case studies in Pascal, CSMP, GPSS and SIMSCRIPT can be found in Neelamkavil.[2]

COLOUR GRAPHICS AND ANIMATION

We are all familiar with the old Chinese proverb 'a picture is worth a thousand words'. Animation makes pictures a thousand times more interesting, aids the manipulation of complex information and improves our understanding of the dynamic behaviour of systems. The colour graphics display of transaction movements and the occurrence of events in a simulation model are extremeley helpful in visualising the operation of the system under normal and abnormal conditions, and several expensive and time-consuming simulation runs can be avoided. SimAnimation and CINEMA provide colour graphics and interactive animation capabilities[2] to the discrete system simulation languages SIMSCRIPT and SIMAN, respectively. RoboTeach is another system used for animated simulations in robotics. Static and animated graphics are becoming standard features in many simulation languages; however, the cost of such systems is still too high. The technology is young and a substantial growth in this field is expected during the next few years.

DISCRETE SYSTEM SIMULATION USING GPSS

General Purpose Simulation System (GPSS) is a flow chart language.[8] Simulation is achieved by creating temporary entities called transactions, moving these transactions through a series of GPSS blocks connected exactly in the same order as the sequence of events and finally removing these transactions from the system. A detailed discussion of GPSS can be found in Bobillier *et al.*[9]

Programming in GPSS can be illustrated by means of a simple example. There are two telephone lines in an office. On average, the office receives 20 phone enquiries every hour; connected calls last 0.033 hours and calls are lost whenever both the lines are busy. It was found that the interarrival time and service time have negative exponential distribution. Thus our problem is to simulate the arrival of 1000 phone enquiries with a view to determining the number of calls lost and the utilisation of the phone lines. Such information will be of great help to the management in planning an efficient and cost-effective telephone system.

The GPSS program below includes comments in each line and is thus self-explanatory:

```
*    EXAMPLE OF A SIMPLE GPSS PROGRAM      * * * * * *
*    SIMULATION OF A PHONE SYSTEM          * * * * * * * *
*    TIME UNIT = 1/1000 HOUR.          * * * * * * * * * * * *
*
        SIMULATE
1       STORAGE      2           NO. OF LINES
1       FUNCTION     RN3,BE      EXPONENTIAL DISTRIBUTION
                                 FOR ARRIVALS
2       FUNCTION     RN4,BE      EXPONENTIAL DISTRIBUTION
                                 FOR SERVICE
        GENERATE     50,FN1      ARRIVAL RATE=20/HOUR
        GATE  SNF    1,LOST      TEST FOR FREE LINES
        ENTER        1,1         ENGAGE ONE LINE
        ADVANCE      33,FN2      SERVICE RATE=30/HOUR
        LEAVE        1,1         SET LINE FREE
        TERMINATE    1           REMOVE CALL FROM SYSTEM
LOST    SAVEVALUE    1+,1        RECORD LOST CALL
```

```
TERMINATE  1        REMOVE CALL FROM SYSTEM
START      1000     SIMULATE 1000 CALLS
END
```

Phone calls are created in GENERATE block and destroyed in TERMINATE block. The lost calls are stored in SAVEVALUE location; the built-in function BE generates samples from exponential distribution using random number generators RN3 amd RN4, and the two phone lines are represented by a STORAGE with capacity 2. Basic statistics are collected automatically by the GPSS system and this includes:

average utilisation of phone lines = 28.83%
number of calls lost   = 115

GPSS is one of the most widely used discrete system simulation languages and both the mainframe and microprocessor versions are available in the market. There are several possible errors in simulation, even if we use a validated model for our simulation experiments. These include errors in the collection, analysis and interpretation of results. Simulation results generally suffer from initial bias and there is no easy way of determining the length of a simulation run and the number of simulation runs required to achieve a specified accuracy of results. Statistical methods in discrete system simulation and ways of detecting and reducing errors are given in Kleijnen.[10]

CONTINUOUS SYSTEM SIMULATION USING CSMP

The purpose of this section is to give a general idea about the nature of programs for simulating continuous systems using a continuous system simulation language (CSSL). The CSMP (continuous system modelling program)[11] for simulating the car suspension system described above is shown below. The purpose of simulation is to select the value of D which minimises the oscillations of the suspension system during a ride on bumpy roads.

```
*   EXAMPLE OF SIMPLE CSMP PROGRAM
*
TITLE CAR SUSPENSION SYSTEM
PARAM D=(.2,.4,25.,55.)
    X2DOT   =(1./M)*(K*F-K*X-D*XDOT)
```

```
XDOT   =INTGRL (.0,X2DOT)
 X   =INTGRL (.0,XDOT)
CONST M=2.,F=1.,K=400.
TIMER DELT=.005,FINTIM=1.5,PRDEL=.05, OUTDEL=.05
PRINT X,XDOT,X2DOT
PRTPLT X
END
STOP
```

The car suspension model is described by lines 5,6,7 of the program; the integration interval for solving the differential equations is defined by DELT; length of simulation is specified by FINTIM; and the interval between printouts and print-plots are described by PRDEL and OUTDEL, respectively. The simulation is repeated for D=.2,.4,25 and 55; the values of X,XDOT and X2DOT are printed with respect to time and the value of X is printed and plotted. A sample of the printout when D = 55 is of the form:

time	X	XDOT	X2DOT
0.0	0.0	0.00	2.00E+2
5.0E−2	1.599E 1	5.0054	3.037E+1
.	.	.	.
.	.	.	.
.	.	.	.
5.5E−1	9.98E−1	3.047E−2	−4.44E−01
.	.	.	.
.	.	.	.
.	.	.	.
1.5	1.0	−1.4959E−7	2.9916E−7

Non-linear properties of the suspension system can be easily introduced into the model and the simulation of non-linear systems do not pose any major problems. This is particularly useful when conventional analytical and numeric methods break down.

SIMULATION ON MICROPROCESSORS
The availability of cheap microprocessors with graphics and software has revolutionised the practice of modelling and

simulation in many fields. There is a growing trend to move away from conventional centralised computing via remote terminals towards distributed local processing using micros and workstations. In several situations, micros can be used as independent single-user systems for model development and simulation. A large number of micro-based simulations using both general purpose and simulation languages have been recently reported.[2]

Discrete system simulation languages, such as GPSS, SIMAN, SIMSCRIPT and SLAM, and continuous system simulation languages, such as ACSL and ISIM, are already available for use on microcomputers. MicroPASSIM, for combined simulation, and InterSIM, an interactive menu-driven simulation package, are also available on micros.

CASE STUDIES IN LARGE-SCALE MODELLING AND SIMULATION

Several large-scale modelling and simulation studies have been carried out in the Department of Computer Science, Trinity College Dublin. A model of the Irish educational system was built,[12] by expressing the future state, ie 5-10 years ahead (enrolments, qualified manpower, emigration, resources available, etc) in terms of the present state of the educational system. An extended version of this model, which rearcasts the past performance of the system, was used to improve the accuracy of the original model. The model gives an estimate of various resource requirements, so that necessary action can be taken well in advance to acquire scarce resources such as finance, teachers and laboratories; if sufficient government funds are not forthcoming to meet the demand or if the educational targets are specified, then the model generates a modified educational plan which satisfies the system constraints. The educational system is described by a 36x36 transition matrix which includes primary, secondary, vocational, teacher training, commercial, technical and third level education, as well as qualified manpower output and emigration.

This model is extremely useful for education planning at both local and national levels. In addition, the study exposed several deficiencies in data collection, analysis and accounting methods and gave a deeper insight into the dynamic behaviour of the education system.

Simulation is probably the most popular method of evaluating new or existing computing systems. A large-scale GPSS-based simulation model of the operating system for the IBM/360 computer was built.[13] The purpose of this study was to investigate the effect of changes in system configurations (eg changes in CPU, discs, memory size, etc) on the performance (response time, throughput, etc) of the overall computer system. Finer details of the OS/360 (including logical sequences of events and operations, and statistical estimates of system parameters) were built into the model and several experiments were conducted using different types of job mixes. The performance of the system under normal and abnormal conditions was studied. The results of the study were extremely useful in identifying system bottlenecks and served as a live exercise in teaching both simulation and computer science.

Another large-scale modelling project in the TCD Department was the development of a model for a production planning system for a local tyre factory.[14] In a large-scale manufacturing environment, customer orders fluctuate continuously and it is impossible to produce a fast, accurate and up-to-date schedule of time-dependent part requirements which are needed for formulating and implementing optimum production policies. Simulation studies are useful in evaluating the implications of shortages of components, the cancellation of orders or the effect of engineering changes on the overall production programme and delivery schedules. In addition, the data provided vital information for forward planning in several areas such as physical planning, financial planning and manpower planning.

There exists strong interaction between various parameters of a manufacturing system and simulation is ideally suited for the study of such systems not only to improve the productivity of the system, but also to understand its dynamics. A large-scale GPSS simulation study was carried out to determine the optimum machine configurations in a local plant of a multinational company which manufactures disposable medical supplies.[15] There are two production lines, each consisting of several machines, and the ON/OFF state of machines are controlled by levels of items in various hoppers which receive the output of different machines. The machine breakdowns are classified into four categories and the characteristics of breakdowns, repair times and machine speed were estimated. Several types of operators, supervisors, foremen and external experts, who operate, repair and maintain the machines, were included in the model. The company was interested not only in optimising the performance of the existing system, but also in designing new systems for future implementation. The results obtained were helpful in identifying the machine and operator configurations which reduced machine-breakdown time, improved machine utilisation and increased the throughput.

In several countries including Ireland, the allocation of university places to students is handled by a central applications office (CAO) at a national level. A copy of the examination results on magnetic tapes is provided by the Department of Education to the CAO, expressing unique preferences for a fixed number of courses out of the total number of courses offered by the various affiliated institutions of the national university system. Based upon their academic and other qualifications, each student is ranked for each of the courses for which a preference has been expressed. A student is said to be eligible for admission to a course if his/her rank is greater than or equal to a specific rank cut-off point for that course. But the actual rank required to gain admission is determined by the demand for that course and the number of places available. The problem is to assign courses to students so as to achieve as high a student-satisfaction rate as possible without violating the system constraints.

A model based on a constrained form of the well-known Stable Marriage problem was developed[16] for optimum assignment of places to students, in the sense that their actual entry standards and the sum of their preferences for the courses assigned are optimised subject to the constraints imposed by the minimum entry standards and the number of places available. The model is particularly useful for simulating the effect of adding new courses, deleting existing courses, lowering entry standards and changing the number of places available on the overall student admissions. The simulation results are useful not only in manpower planning and the formulation of admissions policies, but also in achieving maximum utilisation of university resources.

As a final example, a large-scale bus-operations simulation study was carried out by Ryan,[17] using data collected on CIE (Córas Iompair Éireann) buses operating in Dublin. The model used for the study was the unvalidated bus-operations simulation model (BUSOPS) developed by IBM in England, which was probably the first model to tackle the problem of the congested 'urban corridor' along which passengers are carried by a number of routes. The main entities in the model are buses, passengers and bus queues. The primary output statistic is the average time spent waiting by the passengers who board the bus. The bus-operating environment includes controlled factors such as number and type of buses, schedule of services and fare collection method, while the uncontrolled factors include bus journey time between stops, number of passengers arriving at a stop, the routes they board, number of alighting passengers and time required for boarding and alighting.

The necessary data for the study was collected over the period 18 July 1973 to 3 August 1973. One can have confidence in simulation results only if it can be validated or proved that the model replicates reasonably well what is happening in the real world. In this study, the validation of the underlying assumptions, validation of data and the overall validation of the model were attempted with limited success.[18] The project provided deeper insight into the problem of bus-scheduling, the methodology of model validation and the model itself.

FUTURE DEVELOPMENTS

There is a growing interest in the use of simulation for problem-solving and this shows our confidence in simulation as a problem-solving technique. The developments in new computer designs and high-level languages are bound to bring about wider applications of simulations in several fields. Simulation is more successful in those areas where mature theory is available, which explains why simulation is more widely used in science and engineering. The growing trend towards the application of quantitative methods in economics, management, social, behavioural and environmental sciences indicates that simulation can make significant contributions in these areas as well.

The definition, development and validation of simulation models, as well as the collection, analysis and interpretation of simulation results, must become easier for ordinary users and there is a need for more user-friendly software. The developments in expert systems and object-oriented languages offer promise in resolving some of these difficulties.[19, 20] Unlike conventional software, there is no predetermined sequence of operations to solve a problem and the expert system is required to synthesise suitable operators for a given task. In an expert simulation system, the user would simply declare the goal and the knowledge about the system, and the machine will then come up with the solution. Thus the user need not be an expert in the technical aspects of simulation. This approach has already been used in the design of the rule-oriented simulation system (ROSS), in which a simulation is defined as a series of objects which communicate via messages, which, in turn, trigger certain actions associated with an object.[21]

The question of conceptual problem description is currently receiving a lot of attention and several research projects are directed towards the development of specification languages to assist in the construction and analysis of models.[22] Another area of activity is in establishing concepts and criteria to assess the credibility and acceptability of simulations.[23] Colour graphics and animation provide enhanced visualisation of objects and inject realism into simulations. Dramatic developments are expected in this field and one can expect graphics and animation as standard features in most of the simulation software within the next few years.

Several simulation packages are already available on micros and more are on the way, with several new facilities including voice keyboard, graphic I/O design, screen editor and automatic linking, loading and recompilation of changed modules. The artificial intelligence languages, such as LISP and Prolog, are currently available on several micros. Prolog is ideal for rapid prototyping and goal-oriented simulation modelling. The spread of simulation of large and complex systems is currently constrained by the number-crunching capability of sequential digital computers. NASA's numerical aerodynamical simulation system, using Cray supercomputers, is expected to reach ten billion calculations per second in 1990. These high-speed supercomputers will be used for modelling and simulation research in aerodynamics, weather prediction, genetic engineering and astrophysics. The era of supercomputers and the projected advance in artificial intelligence, graphics, animation, simulation software and distributed systems guarantee an exciting future for simulation and its applications.

CHAPTER 9

An OR Approach to Inflation and Cash Flow

SEAMUS O'CARROLL

Cement-Roadstone Holdings

Between 1968 and 1975, the annual rate of increase in the Consumer Price Index (CPI) rose from 4.5% to 22%. While we were all familiar with inflation in low single figures, double-digit inflation was uncharted territory for the Irish economy and Irish business in particular. Other countries with hard experience had found their own solution: Germany with its 1920s experience controlled inflation at all costs; Brazil institutionalised it by indexing everything. In Britain and Ireland, there was much philosophising and hand-wringing. As inflation climbed towards 20%, one respected investment analyst produced figures to show that no country had pulled back from inflation rates in excess of 20% without violent overthrow of the government. As most of the statistics related to South American countries the relationship was questionable. Was Ireland headed the same way?

By 1974, the problem of how to handle the impact of inflation in evaluating investments and in the day-to-day management of businesses became a serious issue. The Institute of Chartered Accountants had introduced a system of inflation accounting, Current Purchasing Power (CPP), to reflect the effect of inflation on assets and liabilities.

The main feature of CPP accounting was the concept of 'gain on monetary liabilities', ie reduction in real purchasing power of debt in the balance sheet could be reflected as a monetary gain or profit. Thus the bigger the debt, the greater the gain or inflation profit. This was clearly an incentive to borrow as much as possible. While it was accepted that the theory behind CPP may have been plausible, the practical effect was very misleading because the higher a company's gearing or debt/equity ratio, the greater the inflation profits.

In 1974, the then British government set up the Sandilands Commission to devise an acceptable system for inflation accounting. When Sandilands finally reported in September 1975, in addition to listing 22 different definitions for profit, they proposed a more realistic if complex set of inflation-accounting adjustments: Current Cost Accounting (CCA).[1] They also set out an implementation programme, recommending that their system should completely displace the existing Historic Cost Accounting (HCA) method within four years! To say the least, this was controversial. After much discussion and argument, the Institute of Chartered Accountants threw out CCA and two subsequent proposed methods of inflation accounting before realising that the only way to handle inflation was the German solution: to keep it under control.

None of this wrangling among the accountants was much use to the ordinary manager who was grappling with the spiral of costs chasing prices at an accelerating pace. By 1974, inflation was a major problem in the Cement-Roadstone operating companies, particularly where products or raw materials were energy-intensive and the inflation of costs and prices far greater than the CPI as a result of the 1973 oil crisis. Profits may have been on budget, but cash flows were low and debt levels rising. The old tested ratios and rules of thumb were not working. What should be done? We needed to understand how inflation impacted on the operating parameters and the normal measures of performance and control. The problem was examined using the normal accounting methods of projecting profit and loss, funds flow and balance sheets over time to examine the impact of different rates of inflation. The trends were obvious, but what were the relationships and how did they operate? A search of the rapidly growing body of literature on inflation yielded no satisfactory measures for the operating manager. The problem needed to be viewed from a different angle.

It was decided to take a mathematical view of the main accounting statements and the effect of inflation on them. After a short period of doodling, a relatively simple model was developed defining the relationship between profit margin, working capital and inflation.

THE OR MODEL

Assume steady state conditions over two accounting periods with:

- constant sales volumes
- constant margin (m) defined as Profit Before Tax (PBT)/Sales
- Working Cap. ratio (w) = (Stocks + Debtors − Creditors)/Sales
- Capital Expenditure (Cx) for replacement only = Depreciation (d)

Cash Flow = PBT + Depreciation − Work Cap. − Cap. Expend − Tax paid

$$S_1 = S(1+r) = S + Sr$$
$$PBT = mS_1 = mS(1+r)$$
$$Work\ Cap. = w(S_1 - S) = wSr$$
$$Tax\ Paid = 0.5mS$$

where S = sales revenue in year 0
S_1 = sales revenue in year 1
r = inflation rate

Cash Flow = mS (1 + r) + d − wSr − Cx − 0.5mS
= mS (r + 0.5) − wSr

For breakeven Cash Flow, ie Cash Flow = 0
mS (r + 0.5) = wSr and therefore $m = w \times \dfrac{r}{r+0.5}$

This simple relationship defined the margin at which breakeven cash flow would be achieved in terms of working capital ratio and inflation. This was labelled the Critical Margin. To generate 'Free Cash Flow', the Critical Margin would have to be exceeded. While the term 'Free Cash Flow' has been used by others in different contexts, it was felt to be a particularly apt use of the term.

The significance of this relationship becomes obvious when one puts numbers on the variables. With inflation of 20% and working capital to sales ratio of 30%, a not-untypical level in some manufacturing companies, the Critical Margin would be:

$$m = w \times \frac{r}{r + 0.5} = 0.3 \times \frac{0.2}{0.2 + 0.5} = 0.086 \text{ or } 8.6\%$$

Thus the business had to achieve an 8.6% net margin before it generated any cash. If it proposed to pay a dividend, it would have to borrow the money.

Obviously, this model was a bit simplistic and there were many other aspects to consider including:

- the effect of capital allowances in reducing taxes;
- capital expenditure for replacement would normally be greater than depreciation given the history of inflation of capital goods;
- sales volumes and working capital levels fluctuated continuously over time.

The model was extended to take most of these factors into account and a series of individual models was created to reflect the characteristics of the different companies within the Group. One possible use considered at the time was to use them for predicting future cash flow. However, this was not an appropriate use and computer financial simulation models already developed were much more suitable for that purpose.

The real usefulness of the model became apparent when the basic model was presented to the line management in the operating companies. The simple mathematics were quickly assimilated and the relationships between inflation, working capital and growth understood in a way which would have been impossible using the conventional accounting approach. It was demonstrated that for divisions or companies having PBT/Sales ratios:

- on the Critical Margin, there would be no surplus of cash and dividends would have to be paid by borrowing;
- below the Critical Margin, companies would have to increase their profit margin or could reduce working capital in order to generate cash, otherwise debt would continue to grow.

Each company became aware of its Critical Margin and the cash effect of reducing its working capital level. Targets were set to produce Free Cash Flow. Guidelines for coping with the effect of inflation were prepared and circulated internally.

Using the model, it was readily demonstrated that the most relevant measures during periods of high inflation were, and still are, profit margin on sales, working capital ratio and net cash flow.

It was also shown that inflation is financial growth without corresponding growth in production. This growth must be funded to meet increased working capital needs, higher interest rates and the increased cost of investment. Businesses were caught between these cash demands on the one side and the efforts by employees and other groups to protect their positions through wage demands, price control and reduction of credit by stronger suppliers.

A greater understanding was obtained of the mechanics of inflation and its pernicious effects on businesses which by their nature have high working capital levels. While trying to fund their working capital growth, their margins were being squeezed.

The real problem which everybody recognised was that with high inflation, profits were overstated by the Historical Cost Accounting rules; depreciation was understated and the FIFO (first-in, first-out) stock rules created stock profits. This latter problem was recognised by the introduction of stock tax relief in 1975. After twelve years and four different proposed systems, the accounting bodies still have not agreed on a method of accounting for inflation.

The model was also useful in examining how other sectors fared under inflation. While most businesses were losers, there were winners. It can be easily seen that companies with negative working capital would generate cash automatically. The retail sector, buying for credit and selling for cash, is an example. The main beneficiaries were the big supermarket chains. With the purchasing muscle to get the best credit terms and sophisticated systems controlling stocks, they had a cash machine. This was a significant factor in financing the rapid expansion of the big supermarket chains during the 1970s.

DEVELOPMENTS OF THE MODEL

It can be seen that while a business operating at the Critical Margin would have constant debt, it would still be generating retained earnings. Therefore its Debt/Equity ratio would be reducing, thereby increasing its borrowing capacity. Further development of the model identified the margin at which Debt/Equity would remain constant.

Debt/Equity Model
Stagnation occurs when:

$\triangle$Debt (cash deficit) = $\triangle$Equity (retained profits)

$\triangle$Debt = $D_0 - S_0 [m(r+0.5)-wr]$

$\triangle$Equity = $0.5mS_1 = 0.5mS_0(1+r)$

$\triangle$Debt = $\triangle$Equity when $m = w \times \dfrac{r}{1.5r + 1}$

This was called the Supercritical Margin. At this point all profits must be retained to maintain the Debt/Equity ratio at or less than 1, the normal financial limit requested by banks. Below this margin the Debt/Equity ratio would increase. If continued, the point would be reached where borrowing capacity would be exhausted and business would be endangered.

Expanding this model over time produced an expression for the time period to reach a given debt/equity limit in terms of the initial debt and equity, the margin, inflation and working capital.

Debt/Equity Model over Time
Debt in year n:

$D_n = D_0 - S_0[m(r+.5)-wr][1+(1+r) + (1+r)^2+... +(1+r)^{n-1}]$

Equity in year n:

$E_n = E_0 + 0.5mS_0[(1+r) + (1+r)^2 +. . . +(1+r)^n]$

If a company operates continuously below the Supercritical Margin over a period, D_n and E_n will converge and the above equations reduce to:

$E_0 - D_0 = S_0[m(1.5r + 1) - wr] \times (1+r)^n/r$

where $(1+r)^n$ = the inflation index in year 'n';

r = the average rate of inflation over years 1 to n.

Using this relationship a company operating below the Supercritical Margin can estimate the time period (n) before the Debt/Equity ratio reaches 1, from the starting point D_0 / E_0.

While these variations of the model were interesting, they had limited practical application. The important benefits were the improved insight into the impact of inflation on cash flow which was obtained from the first simple model.

CHAPTER 10

OR ECALL* – A Delphi Technique – with memories

MICEÁL ROSS

Economic and Social Research Institute

As I recall, the early meetings of the OR Society were attended by people who were often isolated in their own companies and found little help for their efforts in the literature then available. They came to the meetings to bounce ideas off their friends and to seek their suggestions in tackling the problems set them by management. A good illustration of this interaction was the analysis of an OR man in Bord na Móna. The Bord had three classes of machines for milling the peat which produced granules of 1″, 1½″ and 2″. The bigger granules were cheaper to mill but took longer to dry. The OR man felt that the Bord should settle for one set of machines to reduce the inventory of spare parts and to increase the efficiency of use. His description of his attempts to choose the best size was severely criticised by Dr M D McCarthy (later to become President of University College Cork) for his failure to develop an appropriate grid of Latin squares. A more basic objection was made by the inimitable John Hyland on the grounds of a faulty definition of the problem. His formula was to retain all three sets of machinery, but to develop better weather forecasting. Each set of machines would be optimal over a particular set of weather conditions and he illustrated his argument so tellingly that it still remains vividly in my memory.

Other interventions were more lighthearted. An OR man in Esso was demonstrating his efforts to apply discounted cash flows in his company. His rather complex formulation was

* The early Greek OR forecasters developed ORACLE at Delphi which had the advantage of ambiguity – a feature often valued by management!

eventually reduced to a quadratic equation which he then solved. The only problem was it had two solutions, one negative and one positive. He expressed his bafflement on how to interpret the negative result. Conrad Leser, later Professor in Leeds, spoke with a mischievous gleam in his eye and said that if Esso felt that their cash would be stolen they might like to pay someone to hold it safely for them. He signalled his willingness to accept such a proposal provided the fee was large enough.

Among the formidable panel at the early meetings were Paddy Byrne, with the most razor-sharp contributions from his background with insurance, and John Hyland whose multiple interests included an attempt to apply OR to the design of the perfect house. It was a constant source of amusement to some of us that John's office was in the same building as the Theosophical Society. We felt that he would have been calmly equitable if the spirits of W B Yeats or AE wandered in to discuss with him his theories on the superiority of Norman blood. David Kennedy, currently Chief Executive of Aer Lingus, and his colleague Maurice Foley (now in Guinness Peat Aviation), were leaders of the Aer Lingus team. David's popularity with AGIFORS explained a lot of the IFORS' decision to hold its 1972 International Conference in Dublin; as the OR society was small (about 50 members) and this was only the sixth triennial conference, it spoke volumes for David's charisma.

Early meetings tried to help Aer Lingus with the optimum scheduling of its aircraft and CIE with its train timetable. By this route Fred Ridgway arrived on the scene. Fred is now one of six international Vice-Presidents of IFORS – an honour he holds with another old member, Bob Kavanagh, who as an exile represents Australia. Terry Forsyth, on his return to Ireland, brought his old boss from the Greater London Council (GLC) to a meeting; Ray Ward's entertaining talk contained a clear account of the difficulties of interaction between the OR man and his client manager. After one frustrating interview, in which the manager countered a request for quantitative information by the remark 'How long is a piece of string?' Ray went home and measured all the pieces of string he could find about the house. He found the distribution of their lengths corresponded to a binomial distribution. What his wife said is not recorded.

Ray Ward spoke of how his team had streamlined the GLC invoicing procedures. Finding that very few of the enormous number of bills were for large amounts, they introduced a tiered system with strict control of the larger invoices and sampling procedures of decreasing frequencies as the individual amounts involved became smaller. One faulty invoice was enough to put the offending firm under permanent strict supervision. The simplicity of the solution was out of all proportion to the huge savings the change made possible.

At this stage, the Bank of Ireland team became the dynamic centre of the OR Society with great commitment and efficiency in its affairs, displayed by such popular personalities as Fred Ridgway, Terry Forsyth, Tom Conlon (*see Chapter 4*) and Pat McGorrian.

In these early discussions, the accent was more often on thought and clear problem definition than on technique. A beautiful example of this was Gordon Foster's design of the International Standard Book Number (ISBN) in the 1960s. Gordon (currently Professor of Statistics, TCD; *see also Appendix C)* was asked to design a set of numbers that would be of minimum length and that could be applied uniquely by each publisher without the need to refer to a central agency. Gordon's answer was to allocate code numbers to publishers which related to their volume of output. Large publishers were given few initial numbers and small publishers a code in which all but the last four numbers were fixed. (For example, the large publishing house of Pergamon Press has the fixed ISBN prefix of 0-08 and the next seven figures change with each new title; whereas Mercier Press has a fixed prefix of six figures (0-85342), followed by four figures which change with each new title.) Experience has shown Gordon's ISBN system to be foolproof.

West Churchman's talks to the OR Society have become legendary for the simplicity of their solutions. His most famous account was of the high rise tower in New York where, in spite of the efforts of the architects and engineers, there were innumerable complaints about the time taken by the elevators to reach the clients. The ingenious solution the OR team proposed was to install mirrors near the push buttons, since they observed that fixing one's appearance reduced one's perception of the time taken for the elevator to arrive.

West Churchman also told of the case where a petrol company wished to know whether it should locate filling stations at crossroads if other companies were located there already. The team found that approaching cars must follow one of twelve patterns and that in only three cases was it convenient for the car to stop for petrol on a particular corner. Four different stations at the same crossroads were only in exceptional cases in competition for the same customers.

George Dantzig was another guest speaker provided to the OR Society by courtesy of the Irish Management Institute and the good offices of Tony Moynihan. His Linear Programming and Extensions was the pathbreaker that launched LP, since Stalin had prevented Kantorovich from publishing his work sooner. George's quip to those who said that they enjoyed his book was to ask if they liked the play; this was a reference to the chapter where he dramatised his discovery of the decomposition technique. In his play, one of the characters, A M Dalks, had a name which George said was made up of the initials of America's leading economists. This mischievous remark caused widespread controversy as economists tried to decide which economists he had in mind.

It is hard to realise today what an innovation linear programming and the computer was then. One Irish OR man, Brian Arthur, found himself working for an international consultancy firm in West Germany and was asked to investigate the optimum production allocation of fertiliser manufacture by a German multinational. To his surprise, the multinational seemed unaware of the existence of LP. Brian drew up his matrix and obtained a solution which was not much different from that painstakingly elaborated by the firm's scientists. Brian's solution, nonetheless, represented a significant saving of about one million DM. The client was delighted. Brian then decided to change the criterion from 'profit' to 'post-tax profits'. The results achieved a very large saving by concentrating production in Belgium. However, the General Manager had been manager of the largest German plant which Brian's new solution would close. This plant had a sentimental value for him and not only was the solution rejected but the account was closed! Such human factors were experienced the hard way by practitioners, such as Brian. He is now Professor in Stanford University and engaged in very creative work on the economics of increasing returns to scale – a topic which frightens both Russia's central planners and American free-marketeers by undermining their assumptions.

Undoubtedly, one of the most rewarding events in the history of the OR Society in Ireland was the 1972 IFORS conference. Its 3-year preparation built a great spirit of camaraderie among the organising committee, whose members included Des Byrne, now General Manager of Wavin, and John Lynch, who runs his own firm for security equipment. It established close relationships with the international programming committee, headed by Heiner Müller Merbach, and whose Vice-Chairman was Roy Johnston (*see Chapter 6*) and on which Gordon Foster was a highly respected member. Other members of the group included the immediate Past President of IFORS, the ebullient Alec Lee, then with Rolls Royce, and the President himself, Arne Jensen of Denmark. Arne's dream was to write up the proceedings of the conference in a horse-drawn caravan while plodding dreamily among the stonewalls of Connemara.

Due to the burning of the British Embassy, IFORS would not underwrite the 1972 Conference in the normal way. The Society's willingness to stick its neck out laid the basis for the solvency the Society has enjoyed ever since. Ireland's contribution was from the Department of the Public Service and related to ambulance locations in the west of Ireland – work with which John Cantwell and Brian Lenehan were associated.

For me the highlight of the Conference was the address by President Erskine Childers which he had written himself. His address was so fine that Sir Charles Goodeve turned to me and said that most delegates would envy the Irish Society in having a national president who understood the potential of OR so clearly. President Childers reinforced this assessment when he met the organising committee at Áras an Uachtaráin after the publication of the Conference proceedings. In the hour and a half he spent with the Committee, he frequently pointed to the problems facing Ireland and asked the Society to address themselves to the search for solutions. In particular, he called on the Society to demonstrate the folly of inflation – the chase after a chimera that brought no lasting prosperity but weakened Ireland's competitiveness. This appeal was made at a time when the oil crisis had not yet occurred and when few were aware of these dangers. Truly his untimely death was a great loss to the nation.

My memories of more recent years are fewer and often centre on the annual Conferences. The choice of Longford for one such gathering disconcerted the *Longford Leader* into a startled editorial on the 'quare hawks' that had descended on the town. Athlone was another memorable occasion where the Agriculture Institute wrestled with the parasite cycle of liver fluke in snails and sheep, and Aoileann Ní Gearailt recorded her efforts to improve the Port of Dingle.

One sad memory is conjured up by the ghost of Ciaran O'Kane who was, in the words of Dubliners, a gentleman and a scholar. Ciaran's work on rebuilding burnt-out ghettos in Belfast was an attractive aspect of his commitment to his community. His work on hospitals in Northern Ireland was first class *(see Appendix B)*. Ciaran was one of a number of committed Northerners whom it was a pleasure to meet.

Professor Young and Sally McClean *(see Appendix G)* are others who have never failed in their support. Professor Young's work on the consequences of bunched recruitment in banks and universities was a real eyeopener when he addressed the Society. Seamus O'Carroll *(see Chapter 9)*, who had pioneering work on inflation accountancy to his name, joined my wife Susan and me at the OR Society's 21st anniversary celebrations in the Phoenix Park. The evening was enjoyable, but I became aware that it was time to shuffle on when two young enthusiasts arrived with their little cherub in a carrycot.

The enthusiasm of the present leaders guarantees the continuation of the work of others now more deeply involved in management or academic life – people such as Professor Enda Hession, Dr Jim Crowley, Dr Harry Harrison *(see Appendix E)*, Dr Cathal Lennon and many others. To the young committee of today they may appear as grand old men; to me they seem to be youthful. In fact, the OR Society might like to research why there are fewer old people around nowadays compared with when I joined the OR Society.

Chronicle of the Operations Research Society of Ireland

JULIAN MacAIRT

Trinity College Dublin

Acknowledgement is made to Frank Bannister for giving access to the Society's official records and to Raymond Burke for past issues of the *Bulletin*. Records do not exist for the period 1964-74. A letter published in *The Irish Times* in July 1986 seeking information about the early years drew no worthwhile response. This chronicle is separated into three parts: the principal events arranged by the Society since 1972; lists of papers presented at the Annual Conferences from 1973 to 1986; and the officers elected annually since 1976-77. Abstracts are available for Conference papers for the years 1973-75.

PRINCIPAL EVENTS

1964　　Foundation of the Operations Research Society of Ireland (ORSI). The name was changed in 1985 to Operations Research and Management Science Society of Ireland (ORMSI).

1971　　First Annual Conference, Dundalk.

1972　　ORSI played host to the International Federation of Operations Research Societies (IFORS) in Dublin. Proceedings were later published by North-Holland under the editorship of Dr Miceál Ross of the Economic and Social Research Institute.

1974　　Publication of P Ciaran O'Kane's book *Operational Research* by Pitman. A booklet *OR in Ireland* was published by the Society.

1975　　Presentation of ORSI paper by D Lyons to IFORS in Kyoto, Japan.

1976   *April:* Professor Dooge invited several academics to an informal meeting in Seanad Éireann to hear Ciaran O'Kane present a short summary of the Kennet Report. Mr J Keating, Minister for Industry and Commerce, presided. The Kennet Report was named after Lord Kennet who was invited by the Council of Europe to examine long-term forecasting within the EEC. The idea was to develop alternative scenarios for the EEC thirty years into the future.

October: Address by Dr K Whitaker.

November: First award by the ORSI to a postgraduate student.

December: Newsletter first issued.

1977   *June:* Address by Professor B Walsh, ESRI, on *Estimating the level of job creation requirements in Ireland.*

November: Seminar on *Multicriteria decision-making,* arranged jointly with the Commerce Faculty, UCD. Speakers were Dr E Jacquet-Lagrèze, J Cantwell, Dr D Norton (Department of Political Economy, UCD), Dr J Crowley (Commerce Faculty, UCD) and Dr M Ross.

December: Address by Professor W Grudzewski, Dean of the Faculty of Computer Science and Management, Technical University of Wroclaw, Poland, on *The role of the OR specialist in a planned economy.*

1978   *February:* Address by Dr M O'Donoghue, Minister for Economic Planning and Development.

March: Dr C O'Kane appointed delegate to IFORS. Dr C Lennon presented paper to IFORS; this showed that about 19% of a sample of patients in Limerick Regional Hospital could have been treated elsewhere.

May: Constitution of the ORSI revised. The two categories of membership – full and associate – were thereafter combined. The Constitution now stated, 'Full membership of the Society shall be open to all who are interested in operations research.'

Also, multivariate analysis course. Speakers were Dr O Egan (Education Research Centre, Drumcondra), Professor M Moran (UCC), Ms June Ryan (IPA) and Dr M Stuart (TCD, Coordinator).

June: Dr H Harrison won first prize at joint TIMS/ ORSA meeting in New York for his paper *A planning system for facilities and resources in distribution networks.*

October: Address by Dr M Dando, Sussex University, on *The failure of strategic management to cope with crises.*

1979   *January:* Joint course with Institute of Chartered Accountants in Ireland on *Application of modelling to financial decisions.* Speakers were Professor P Rivett (Sussex University), Mr E McDonnell and S O'Carroll (Cement-Roadstone), J Kelly (IDA) and Mr D Kennedy (Aer Lingus, Chairman).

March: Address by Dr D Carroll.

August: ORSI's *Bulletin* launched under the editorship of Dr J Crowley.

November: Special lecture series on *Planning for a Papal Visit.* Speakers were Rev Fr Fehilly (Director of Operations), Mr E Doherty (Assistant Commissioner, Garda Síochána), Mr P Darmody (Assistant General Manager – Operations, CIE), Capt J Millar (Press Officer, Aer Lingus) and Mr P Gleeson (Senior Producer, RTE). The visit of His Holiness was essentially a pastoral exercise for the Church. But the planning and management of facilities for large-scale crowd movement and control, for multi-location media coverage and swift movement of the Papal entourage was an exercise in logistics on a grand scale.

December: Launching of Dr Tom O'Donovan's book, *GPSS: Simulation made simple.*

1980   *March:* Address by Mr Fred O'Connell, Nielsen.

April: Address by Mr Albert Reynolds, Minister for Telecommunications.

1981   *August:* P Herlihy presented paper to IFORS on *The use of OR in the revision of constituencies for Dáil Éireann.*

November: Address by Mr Martin Flinter, Aer Lingus, on *Airmotive Ireland.*

December: Address by Mr Padraic White, Head of IDA, on *Planning for industrial development.*

1982   *April:* Course on *Linear programming.*

May: Seminar on *Business applications of microcomput-*

ers. Speakers were Mr M Butler (UCD), F Bannister, T Conlon, B Flanagan (P.E. Ltd), J Conroy (Price Waterhouse), D Notley (Notley-Cahill Consulting), M Ryan (NIHED), R Faulkner (Rainsford Logistics) and P O'Beirne (Systems Modelling).

June: Two regional members elected to Council of the ORSI: Dr T O'Donovan (UCC) and Dr R Gault (UCG).

October: Address by Dr R Gault on *The scope of OR methodology.*

November: Address by Bob Kavanagh, Swinburne Institute, Melbourne, on *OR in Australia.*

1983   *February:* Address by Mr M Boyle, Assistant Chief Executive, Bord Gais, on *The Cork-Dublin pipeline.*

March: Seminar on *Time series analysis* by Dr A Raftery, TCD.

April: Seminar on *OR in the health services.* Speakers were from Stokes Kennedy Crowley, Health Services OR Unit, Strathclyde University, Exeter University and N.E. Thames Regional Health OR Unit, London.

May: Seminar on *Use of APL computer language* by the firm Cocking & Drury. Part of the seminar was devoted to describing the language and a discussion of its advantages and disadvantages, augmented by applications.

1984   *February:* Address by Professor Brian Haley on *Forgotten theories of OR.*

March: Address by T Conlon on *FORSSIGHT.*

Also, address by S Condon of Córas Tráchtála on *Selling consultancy services overseas.*

April: Address by Professor Kieran Kennedy on *National integrated planning.*

Also, course on *Microcomputers in production and inventory control.* Speakers were F Bannister, D Gannon (IMI), A Dromgoole (SKC), M Pierce (Mentec International) and F Cole (Manufacturing Management Systems).

May: Development Plan issued for the ORSI.

August: H Harrison and F Bannister presented papers

to IFORS entitled, respectively, *Restructuring for improved efficiency in the agribusiness sector of the Irish economy* and *Decision support systems – New opportunities for OR.*

November: Address by Mr T Hardiman of the National Planning Board.

1985   *January:* The ORSI instituted two awards at the Annual Aer Lingus Young Scientists' Exhibition – a group award and an individual award. (This innovation was based on Bob Kavanagh's Australian experience.) The group winner was a team from Presentation Convent, Thurles, for a project concerned with reducing electricity costs at Holycross Abbey. The individual winner was a student from Douglas Community School, Cork, for a project entitled *Early detection of haybarn fires.*

March: Seminar on *Simulation.* Speakers were T Conlon (B of I), M Ó hÉigeartaigh (NIHED), A Mullarney (CACI), T O'Donovan (UCC) and M Brady (Price Waterhouse, Coordinator).

May: Address by Mr M Keating, TD, Chairman of the Oireachtas Committee on State Expenditure.

June: Constitution of the ORSI revised and title altered to 'Operations Research & Management Science Society of Ireland' (ORMSI). The term of future Presidents extended to two years.

Also, 21st Birthday Party of the ORMSI at the Phoenix Park Racecourse.

1986   *February:* Submission made to Oireachtas Committee on Small Businesses (see *Bulletin,* Autumn 1986).

AGENDA OF ORMSI ANNUAL CONFERENCES

Athlone, 1973:

A Bean Mhic Gearailt and R Johnston, TCD, *A Study in the development of a fishing centre.*

J Cantwell, Government OR Unit, *Resource Allocation for forest fire protection.*

B Carroll, T Conlon, P Herlihy and R Johnston, TCD, *Bulk*

milk collection by Lough Egish Co-operative Society.

B Feeney and A Metcalf, CIE, *Behavioural modelling in price analysis.*

C Geltenby, NUU, *Assessment of the effectiveness of control techniques for liver fluke infection.*

J Glass and E Kiountouzis, NUU, *Mathematical programming models for national planning.*

H Harrison, UCD, *An integrated route planning and control system by computer.*

D Lyons, TCD, *Depot location.*

T McGovern, Systems Dynamics, *Producing a model of bank personnel structure.*

H Perros, TCD, *Computer performance evaluation.*

M Ross, ESRI, *Decentralised planning.*

C Tynan, C Garvan, F Ó Muircheartaigh and M Franklin, TCD, *Factors affecting profitability in pig fattening.*

Longford, 1974:

A Bean Mhic Gearailt and B Lenehan, DPS, *Siting of chips.*

J Bradley, IIRS, *Development of polynomial programming techniques with application to the building industry.*

J Cantwell, Government OR Unit, *Manpower planning for telephone development.*

G Franklin and R Johnston, TCD, *A national planning model for qualified manpower in Ireland.*

F G Foster and H Perros, TCD, *A simple analytic approach to computer performance evaluation.*

M Heaton, RTC Carlow, *A fast-reaction, self-modifying forecast method.*

C Lennon, SKC, *A corporate planning model of the Irish sea fishing industry.*

D Lyons, TCD, *The mix-feed problems.*

C O'Kane, QUB, *The operation of a hospital paramedical department – An empirical investigation.*

J Potts and N Honeyman, Government OR Unit, *Resource requirements in Colleges of Technology.*

E Mullins, P O'Mahony and M Stuart, TCD, *A computer model of the Irish tax and social welfare system.*

Galway, 1975:

R Gault, UCG, *Hospital nursing requirements.*

C Lennon, SKC, *Determination of bed population ratios for acute care hospitals.*

E O'Kelly, J Roche and R Gault, UCG, *Statistics and the law.*

T O'Donovan, UCC, *New techniques in queueing theory.*

J Haslett, TCD, *Preliminary models for the storage of solar energy.*

E Henry, ESRI, *Input-output models of energy supply and demand in Ireland.*

M Walsh, *Business applications of catastrophe theory.*

J Cantwell, DPS, *A review of the activities of the Government Operations Research Unit and some lessons learned.*

L O'Reilly, Central Bank, *Methods of estimating quarterly national accounts.*

M O'Regan, Educational Research Council, and L Daly, Government OR Unit, *The gift of bilocation.*

E Sugrue, UCG, *Manning requirements of our Irish docks.*

S O'Carroll, Cement-Roadstone, *Cash flow models with inflation.*

F G Foster and H Perros, TCD, *A computer performance evaluation exercise carried out on ALT real-time computer system ASTRAL.*

Dublin, 1977:

T Abodunde, NUU, *Recruitment policies and production planning.*

M Clancy and P Herlihy, AFT, *The measurement of muscle size.*

J Crowley, UCD, *Operational features of potential containerised freight transport systems.*

H Harrison, UCD, *A dynamic corporate planning model.*

J Killen, TCD, *Minimum waiting time schedule for the Dublin suburban railway.*

C Lennon*, SKC, *Classification of patient needs in an acute care hospital.*

S McClean, NUU, *Continuous time stochastic models.*

M Walsh, *Integrated OR systems.*

J Markham, CIE, *Nothing is better than data.*

L Walshe and M McConnell, UCD, *Optimisation of building design.*

J Haslett, TCD, *Models in solar water heating: A critical comparison.*

*Chosen to represent the ORMSI at IFORS 1978.

Dundalk, 1978:

D Lyons, Bord Bainne, *Linear programming – A financial model.*

T Conlon, Bank of Ireland, *Discounted cash flow, investment in equipment and Irish taxation.*

J Faulkner, Guinness, *Simulation in practice – A case study at Guinness.*

W McCarthy, DPS, *Foreign exchange – Snake and arbitage.*

T Conlon, Bank of Ireland, *An OR opportunity in banking.*

J Timlin, Allied Irish Banks, *Manpower planning in AIB.*

S McClean, NUU, *Entropy as a measure in manpower planning systems.*

T O'Donovan, UCC, *An approach to teaching simulation using GPSS.*

R Johnston, TCD, *The interface between university and industry.*

A Buttimer, *Presenting the results.*

B Carroll, TCD, *A study in nutrition.*

J Haslett, TCD, *Solar energy systems modelling.*

R Kavanagh, DPS, *Forecasting energy requirements.*

Cork, 1979:

R Kavanagh, NBST, *Energy model for Ireland.*

D Tocher, NIHE, *An examination of the criteria used in deciding how many nurses in a clinical area.*

A Unwin, TCD, *Decision rules.*

N Reid, NUU, *An OR approach.*

M Hegarty, College of Commerce, Rathmines, *Mathematical programming applied to energy forecasting.*

J Brandrick, *Quality control in Braun.*

M Kenny, NET, *Production scheduling in NET's Cork plant.*

D O'Cinnéide, UCC, *The Cork business communications study.*

A Young, NUU, *Minimum time required to meet desirable manpower objectives.*

M O'Beirne, NET, *Prophet: a corporate planning model.*

B Carroll, NBST, *Work of National Board for Science and Technology.*

Limerick, 1980:

J Haslett, TCD, *Modelling the implications of large-scale windpower generation for electricity grids.*

E Kelledy, TCD, *The Irish contribution to the EEC solar energy*

R&D effort.

B Sweeney, ALT, *Inter-airline ticket sampling – Some current developments.*

D O'Connor, UCD, *Approximate completion time distributions in PERT networks.*

R Burke, SKC, *A socio-economic computer model for regional planning.*

P Herlihy, AFT, *L. P. techniques and forecasting sow numbers.*

S McClean, NUU, *Study of the growth of credit unions in Ireland.*

C O'Kane, QUB, *An OR application to the hospital service.*

R Cochrane, NBST, *Assessing the implication of microelectronics for the Irish economy.*

F O'Mahony, College of Commerce, Rathmines, *Non-rational decision-making.*

T White, NCEA, *OR education in Regional Colleges.*

R Johnston, TCD, *An analytical approach to biomass production and conversion to energy in Ireland.*

GUEST SPEAKERS: T Ryan, Chief Executive of Guinness Peat Aviation, and B Robinette, Managing Director of Mostek Ireland.

Athlone, 1981:

C Ní Bhriain, Department of Post and Telegraphs, *Forecasting the demand for telecommunications.*

P McClean, QUB, *Queueing in the accident emergency department, Royal Victoria Hospital.*

J MacAirt, TCD, *A national schoolmeals system at minimum cost.*

B O'Connor, Aer Rianta, *Short-term forecasting of air passenger traffic.*

A Unwin, TCD, *Stability conditions for single-queue systems.*

S Reagan, *Use of a microcomputer in materials requirement planning.*

P Herlihy, AFT, *Application of L.P. to estimating the pig breeding herd.*

W McAleer, QUB, *Activity analysis in estimating the demand for energy in Northern Ireland.*

GUEST SPEAKER: E O'Kelly of Department of Industrial Engineering, UCG.

Kilkenny, 1982:

B Lenehan and J Reilly, DPS, *Forecasting age and experience structures in the Irish civil service.*

M Sheridan, Department of Post and Telegraphs, *Computer-aided planning in the Irish telecommunications network.*

J Crowley, UCD, *Vehicle scheduling – A case study.*

E Ring, Sligo RTC, *Load planning in Travenol Laboratories.*

M Brady, Price Waterhouse, *Discrete systems simulation with SIMSCRIPT.*

F Bannister and M McCarthy, Price Waterhouse, *From calving to cash flow: Simulating a creamery farm.*

J Harken, Digital, Clonmel, *A soft approach to project management.*

GUEST SPEAKER: P O'Neill, Assistant CEO, Avonmore Creameries Ltd, Kilkenny.

Galway 1983:

B Sloan, TCD, *Computer simulation – Some statistical issues.*

S McClean, NUU, *Control theory for manpower planning.*

H Harrison, UCD, *Structural reorganisation in warehousing and distribution.*

C O'Kane, QUB, *A micro answer to the nurse rota problem.*

P Herlihy, AFT, *Modelling the effect of changes in the frequency of collection on the direct energy requirements of milk assembly.*

A Unwin, TCD, *OR modelling for PR voting.*

F Bannister, Price Waterhouse, *Decision support systems – New opportunities for OR.*

T Gibbons, TCD, *In search of the golden rule: A dynamic programming formulation.*

GUEST SPEAKER: Frank Flynn, Chief Executive of Údarás na Gaeltachta.

Dundalk, 1984:

C Murphy, UCG, *Measuring the cost of violence in Northern Ireland.*

S McClean, NUU. *Sampling nurses in different age groups.*

P Herlihy, AFT, *Optimum truck sizes for milk co-operatives.*

I Williams, NIHE, *Model of freight traffic through Buenos Aires port.*

I Naqvi, QUB, *A dynamic programming approach to a multi-*

dimensional assortment problem.
M Ross, ESRI, *Measuring the numbers employed in the civil service.*
M Byrne, Price Waterhouse, *Darwinism and OR.*
M Ó hÉigeartaigh, NIHED, *Proposals for a national software centre.*
F Bannister, Price Waterhouse, *Fourth generation modelling language.*

Dublin, 1985:
S McClean, UU, *Extended use of entropy in manpower planning.*
B Lenehan, DPS, *Manpower planning revisited.*
R Johnston, TCD, *Enterprise development and the third level system.*
M Butler, UCD, *Vehicle routing problem.*
R Kavanagh, Bord na Móna, *Towards a strategic framework.*
C Murphy, UCG, *Whither OR?*
D Lyons, TCD, *Management science software.*
M Ó hÉigeartaigh, NIHED, *Estimating knot volumes in wood.*

Dublin, 1986:
L Killen, AFT, *Optimal grassland management – A linear programming model.*
S Ward, Bord na Móna, *Milled peat production operations.*
W McAleer, QUB, *A study of a dental school.*
R Bates, Meteorological Service, *Models and weather forecasting.*
L Daly, UCD, *Angina and Markov processes.*
P McClean, SKC, *OR developments in the UK and parallels for Ireland.*

Dublin, 1987:
A Cater, UCD, *Artificial intelligence.*
T MacEochagain, Peregrine, *BRIGADE.*
F Bannister, Price Waterhouse, *Practical implications of expert systems.*
P Henry, TCD, *Integrating AI technology with OR practice.*
J Currie, UCG, *Expert systems in accounting and tax.*
M Butler, UCD, *Vehicle scheduling.*
S Ward and P O'Kane, UCD, *Milled peat drying model.*
P Herlihy, AFT, *Modelling beef production enterprises.*
M Fahy, UCG/SKC, *DSS for financial services marketing.*
A Unwin, TCD, *Interactive graphics package for time series analysis.*

OFFICERS OF THE ORMSI FROM 1976-77 TO 1986-87

Year	President	Vice-President	Secretary	Treasurer
1976-77	M Ross *(ESRI)*	D Byrne *(Guinness)*	T Conlon *(B of I)*	D Lyons *(Bord Bainne)*
1977-78	J Cantwell *(DPS)*	T Conlon	F Bannister *(DPS)*	C Lennon *(SKC)*
1978-79	T Conlon	C Lennon	F Bannister	L Daly *(UCD)*
1979-80	C Lennon	R Faulkner	F Bannister	L Daly
1980-81	R Faulkner	J Crowley *(UCD)*	M Ó hÉigeartaigh *(College of Commerce, Rathmines)*	F Bannister
1981-82	J Crowley	C O'Kane *(QUB)*	F Bannister *(Price Waterhouse)*	A Unwin *(TCD)*
1982-83	C O'Kane	F Bannister	L Killen *(AFT)*	E McColl *(TCD)*
1983-84	F Bannister	T Gibbons *(TCD)*	M Brady *(Price Waterhouse)*	P McClean *(SKC)*
1984-85	M O'Regan *(TCD)*	B Lenehan *(DPS)*	M Brady	P McClean
1985-86	B Lenehan	R Kavanagh *(Bord na Móna)*	P McClean	J MacAirt *(TCD)*
1986-87	R Kavanagh	P McClean	M Maguire *(Kevin St. College)*	J MacAirt
1987-88	R Kavanagh	P McClean	M Maguire	J MacAirt

OR in Queen's University Belfast (QUB)

W E McALEER

Professor Harry Harrison, now of UCD, was the first lecturer in quantitative methods in QUB's Department of Business Studies and was appointed soon after the Department was founded in 1965. Courses in OR and business statistics were essential elements of the post-graduate Diploma in Business Administration (DBA) which was the first qualification offered by the Department. Ciaran O'Kane, a civil engineer, was a student on the first DBA course in 1967 and joined Harrison as a lecturer soon after. Course development in the early years was influenced by interests in linear programming (blending of Bushmills' whiskey was one involvement) and by the training of O'Kane at the M.Sc. course in statistics and OR at TCD.

Harrison left in 1971 and the author, an electrical engineer with work experience in the USA, was appointed. The major course developments in the early and middle 1970s were the introduction of an undergraduate degree with OR and statistics as core courses and the offering of options on the MBA programme, so that post-graduate students had the opportunity of more advanced courses in addition to the core courses. These options were linear programming, sampling, inventory control, simulation and forecasting. After 1975, only two options were offered – systems modelling and OR.

The interests of O'Kane in the application of OR in health services and of the author in energy modelling and the methodology of OR were reflected in course content and developments. Of particular relevance was the establishment of the Health and Social Services Management Research Unit in 1979, funded by the Eastern Health and Social Services Board (EHSSB) in Northern Ireland, with O'Kane as the

Director of the Unit. He continued in this position until his untimely death in 1984. During that time, the Unit was involved in many projects. The EHSSB were anxious that the work of the Unit should continue and the author is now its Director.

The main course developments of the 1980s have taken place since 1984, when QUB established a School of Management and Finance, consisting essentially of the departments of accounting and business studies. Courses in statistics and OR and management information systems (MIS) based on the use of computers in business are now core courses on the B.Sc. (Management) degree. Mary Kane, an applied mathematician with considerable experience of the commercial use of computers, joined the Department of Business Studies in 1984. Since then she has been very influential in the design of MIS courses and the establishment of a computer laboratory based on IBM and Apple micros with communication facilities to the university's mainframe computers.

The latest course development has been the redesign of the MBA programme so that it can be taken full-time in one year or part-time (4.30-7.30pm) over three years. The syllabus has also been redesigned, from October 1986. The emphasis on management science in the core has decreased due to the need to include a core course on computers and MIS. The options now depend on the availability of staff (due to university cutbacks, Dr O'Kane's post in QUB has not been filled). By government decision, all MBA courses in Northern Ireland after 1987-88 will be in the University of Ulster.

RESEARCH PAPERS

McAleer, W. E. Which methodology. *UK Systems Society Newsletter,* Vol. 6, 1981, pp. 3-5.

McAleer, W. E. *The demand for energy in Northern Ireland – An activity analysis approach.* ORSI Annual Conference, 1981 (unpublished).

McAleer, W. E. Systems: A concept for business and management. *Journal of Applied Systems Analysis,* Vol. 9, 1982, pp. 99-129.

McAleer, W. E. An end-use energy demand forecasting model

for Northern Ireland. *5th European Conference OR and 25th International Meeting of Institute of Management Sciences,* Lausanne, 1982, No. 2232, p. 17.

McAleer, W. E. A regional and use energy demand model. *Omega,* Vol. 10, No. 6, 1982, pp. 629–639.

McAleer, W. E. The domestic sector demand for fuels in Northern Ireland. *Journal of IBAR,* Vol. 4, No. 2, 1982, pp. 58–71.

McAleer, W. E. *OR/MS methodologies – A criticism of the rush to mathematical models.* 6th European Congress on OR, Vienna, 1983 (unpublished).

McAleer, W. E., Kane, M.W. and Naqvi, I. A study of the operation of the dental school. *Health and Social Services Management Research Unit (MRU),* QUB, No. 2, 1985, p. 30.

McAleer, W. E., Moore, A. and Naqvi, I. The catchment area of the Ulster Hospital, Dundonald. *MRU,* No. 1, 1986, p. 13.

O'Kane, P. C. *et al.* A simulation experiment using two languages. *Computer Journal,* Vol. 23, No. 2, 1980, pp. 142–146.

O'Kane, P. C. *OR applied to hospital activities.* 4th European Congress OR, Cambridge, 1980 (unpublished).

O'Kane, P. C., McClean, P. and Sheppard, C. R. An investigation into methods of decreasing patient waiting time in the accident and emergency department of the Royal Victoria Hospital. *MRU,* No. 2, 1980, p. 71.

O'Kane, P. C. and McClean, P. Ambulance maintenance policy – Design of a management information system. *MRU,* No. 8, 1980, p. 17.

O'Kane, P. C. and Hamilton, P. A commentary on existing nurse rota systems in two hospitals in the North and West Belfast districts. *MRU,* No. 3, 1981, p. 33.

O'Kane, P. C., McClean, P. and Sheppard, C. R. Survey of night-time demand for emergency ambulances. *MRU,* No. 1, 1981, p. 10.

O'Kane, P. C. *Two contrasting manpower scheduling projects.* 7th Annual Meeting Dur. Work. Group on OR Appl. to Health Services, Trondheim, 1981 (unpublished).

O'Kane, P. C. and Boldy, D. Health OR – A selective overview. *EJOR,* Vol. 10, 1982, pp. 1–9.

OR in Trinity College Dublin (TCD)

F G FOSTER

Training in OR commenced in Trinity College in 1969 with the introduction of the M.Sc. in Statistics and Operations Research, administered by the Department of Statistics. The development of this degree programme followed on from a national survey, carried out by a working group of the OR Society, on the need for such training and on employment opportunities in Ireland. The group estimated that the intake of graduates in this field into Irish industry and public services would be around 12 per annum. The programme was set up to supply this need.

The Department of Statistics itself was set up in Trinity College in 1967 with the appointment of the author to the Chair. In 1969, the staff consisted of Julian MacAirt, Aidan Moran and Michael Franklin. For part-time teaching assistance on the programme, members of the OR Society and others were called on.

The Department has expanded fairly rapidly since that time. Further staff recruited to the Department since 1969 were Bob Kavanagh (1970), Edward Minieka (1971-72, Visiting Professor), Ailsa Land (1971-72, Donegall Lecturer), Sarah Davis (1972), Michael Stuart (1972), Roy Johnston (1972, Research Associate), John Haslett (1973), Sean O'Broin (1975, part-time), Robert Dummer (1976), Kris Mosurski (1977), Patrick Herlihy (1977, part-time), Patrick Perry (1977, part-time), Brian Sweeney (1977, part-time), Antony Unwin (1978), Christian Agunwamba (1978, Visiting Lecturer), Eamonn Mullins (1979), Sue Humphries (1979), Trevor Gibbons (1980), Adrian Raftery (1980), Myra O'Regan (1981), Eileen Drew (1981), Elaine McColl (1982, Statistical Programmer), Heather Ruskin (1982, part-time), Donal Lyons (1984, part-time), Patrick O'Beirne (1985, part-time), Michael Walsh (1985, part-time) and Ray Crotty (1985, Research Associate).

The M.Sc. degree programme was planned from the start to have a problem-orientation. A substantial proportion of the students' time was to be devoted to the study of a real practical problem and to the writing of a report on this problem. In this connection, sponsored projects were carried out for State bodies, private industry and the civil service. These projects were normally worked on jointly by groups of two or three students under staff supervision. A vast number of such projects have been carried out over the years in very many different fields, such as manufacturing, transport, health, forestry, agriculture, fisheries, brewing and nutrition. Reports on these studies are kept in the Departmental library. Being problem- or mission-orientated, these studies tended naturally to be multi-disciplinary, so that academic distinctions between 'disciplines', such as 'statistics' or 'OR', did not arise. (Indeed the author would have reservations about the usefulness of such distinctions in this context.)

To coordinate these activities and also to assist in the dissemination and application of statistical and OR techniques in Ireland, the Statistics and Operations Research Laboratory was established in 1972 as a section of the Department. The Laboratory undertakes the analysis and execution of research projects for departments of the College and also for outside bodies. Roy Johnston was associated with the Laboratory in the earlier years and played a key role in identifying clients and processing projects in connection with the M.Sc. degree programme.

It should be mentioned that OR instruction was also provided in the evening Diploma in Statistics which was set up in 1970 and which is still in operation.

Following on from discussions with the Government Department of Finance, a further M.Sc. degree programme was introduced in 1973. The Public Sector Analysis programme is inter-disciplinary and was specifically tailored to the needs of those involved in the broad field of planning and analysis in the public sector. Students on this programme are normally seconded from Government departments and the aim of the programme is specifically directed towards developing the analytical abilities of such students for application to the range of problems confronting their departments, so that they will be capable of both seeing the full ramifications of public policy as well as being able to use the techniques, quantitative and qualitative, appropriate to the particular economic and social issues with which they may be involved.

A further significant development was the inception in 1977 of the Systems Development Programme. This one-year M.Sc. degree programme was funded as an integral part of the Government Department of Foreign Affairs Bilateral Aid Programme of technical assistance to developing countries. It was intended for nationals of developing countries on secondment from their organisations. Participants have included officers of government departments, managers in business, finance and social institutions, and teachers and researchers from universities. A proposal for the study of a specific development problem from each applicant endorsed by the employing organisation is one of the conditions of acceptance. This in-depth study, carried out in the spirit of OR and applying the analytical tools learned during course work, constitutes the central part of the programme. A report on it is written under the guidance of a tutor and with individual consultation from appropriate Irish development agencies. The report is intended to be of direct use on the participant's return home. Areas of study have included agriculture, banking, electricity generation, health, educational planning, export promotion, industrial development, informatics, manpower planning, project appraisal, telecommunications and transport. A large number of these reports are available in the Departmental library.

More recent significant developments have been the incorporation of TCD's Department of Statistics into the School of Systems and Data Studies within the Faculty of Engineering and Systems Sciences, and the creation within this School of a four-year undergraduate moderatorship in Management Science and Industrial Systems Studies (MSISS).

The MSISS degree programme commenced in 1980. It was set up as part of TCD's response to Government requests at that time to meet the shortage (identified by the Industrial Development Authority) of graduates in engineering and related disciplines. Its syllabus reflects current trends in OR towards increasing concern with information systems and the use of the personal computer for problem-solving. It is multi-disciplinary and problem-oriented.

Although the programme is centred on management science, other disciplines provide necessary background, so that careers not directly related to industrial management are also possible for our graduates, such as teaching, the civil service, State-sponsored bodies and hospital administration. To date, two cohorts have graduated and while, inevitably on account of the changed economic climate, only a minority have found jobs in Ireland, the vast majority have obtained satisfying jobs either here or abroad. A number are with consultancy firms.

During the years while the MSISS programme was completing its first full four-year cycle, the M.Sc. programme in Statistics and OR was put in abeyance in order to concentrate staff resources on the considerable task of developing the new moderatorship. Now that this transient phase has passed, the most recent development has been the re-introduction in 1986 of the M.Sc. in a new form. Students may now read for either an M.Sc. in Management Science or an M.Sc. in Statistics. The new feature of these programmes is that they are research-oriented and the intention is that students will participate in on-going staff research projects. Within these projects they will be assigned individual research studies together with course work.

TCD graduates in the OR field hold positions – some now very senior – in all sectors of Irish industry, commerce and the public service. They are too numerous to name. Many are contributors to this book.

OR in University College Cork (UCC)

TOM O'DONOVAN

The Statistics Department provides all of the courses in Operations Research that are currently being taught in UCC. The main service course in OR is MGT201 Quantitative Methods for Management. This course, which has been in existence since 1977, is now a compulsory unit for Third Year Commerce students and for UCC's Second Year Honours students in the Faculties of Arts and Science. It may also be selected as an option by Third and Fourth Year Civil Engineering students. A comparable course is available as an option for Third Year Computer Science students.

The topics covered in the course include linear and integer programming, network flow models, decision analysis, simulation, heuristic methods and project management. The course consists of 50 lectures and 12 practical sessions in the microcomputer centre. Approximately 160 students attend the course each year.

Since 1985, a service course on quality control has been introduced, entitled S3.1 Statistical Methods and Quality Control. This course is available as an option for Third Year General Science students. Approximately 10 students avail of this option each year.

UCC's Honours courses for Third Year Arts and Science students include SH3.3 Stochastic processes; SH3.4 Time Series; and SH3. 11 Theory of Operational Research. Queueing theory and simulation using GPSS are included in SH3.3.

DEPARTMENT PUBLICATIONS BY THE AUTHOR
The queue M/G/1 with the semipreemptive priority queueing discipline. *Operations Research,* Vol. 20, No. 2, 1972, pp. 434-439.

Distributions of attained and residual service in general queueing systems. *Operations Research,* Vol. 22, No. 3, 1974, pp. 570-575.

Direct solutions of M/G/1 processor-sharing models. *Operations Research,* Vol. 22, No. 6, 1974, pp. 1232-1235.

The queue M/G/1 when jobs are scheduled within generations. *Operations Research,* Vol. 23, No. 4, 1975, pp. 821-824.

Conditional response times in M/M/1 processor-sharing models. *Operations Research,* Vol. 24, No. 2, 1976, pp. 382-385.

Direct solutions of M/G/1 priority queueing models. *Revue Française d'Automatique Informatique et Recherche Operationelle,* Vol. 10, No. 2, 1976, pp. 107-111.

GPSS: Simulation made simple. Wiley, Chichester and New York, 1979.

Short-term forecasting: An introduction to the Box-Jenkins approach. Wiley, Chichester and New York, 1983.

Review of 'Simulation and the Monte Carlo Method' by R. Y. Rubenstein. *Biometrics,* Vol. 39, No. 1, 1983, p. 302.

VisiCalc made simple. Wiley, Chichester and New York, 1984.

OR in University College Dublin (UCD)

HARRY HARRISON

The Department of Management Information Systems within the Faculty of Commerce at UCD was established in 1980 on the filling of the Chair by the author. The Department currently has five full members of staff and 20 tutors and demonstrators. The teaching spans all three years of the undergraduate courses in Commerce, the subject being denoted a core, or compulsory, subject. In addition the Department runs the University's Business Microcomputer Centre, which has 100 microcomputers.

The undergraduate courses in Management Information Systems are divided evenly between Management Science and Business Computing, except for an advanced course in Optimisation which is offered in the final year as an optional additional subject. The courses in Management Science cover both probability theory and applied statistics, as well as mathematical programming, queueing theory, simulation and the like.

At graduate level, the Department is heavily involved in various masters' degree courses which include: Business Administration (MBA), Public Administration (MPA), Business Studies (MBS) and Management Science (M Mangt Sc).

The Master of Management Science degree programme is an extremely rigorous course of study in many advanced topics in Operations Research and Data Processing. This degree programme admits not only high-quality graduates in commerce, but also in mathematics, engineering and the sciences. A typical yearly enrolment is twenty.

The Department is active in research and members have published many papers in international journals, as well as being invited speakers at international conferences. For instance, the author delivered an invited paper in Brisbane in 1986 for the TIMS XXVII International Conference. The late Dr Patrick F Perry, the Director of the Management Science Degree Programme, made a study visit to the Signal Theory and Processing Group of the Polytecnica University of Madrid (Spain's foremost technical university institution), also in 1986. This Group has research interests concentrating on digital signal processing theory and application in radar, sonar, communication and speech. Latest developments in control theory for large-scale dynamic systems optimisation, with particular emphasis on process and factory automation, were presented during the visit.

Dr A Deegan, Director of UCD's Business Microcomputer Centre, has a background in computer-based information systems, with an emphasis on database applications. He has been involved in many projects involving university/industry co-operation which centre on the development of data bases to support commercial applications, many of which have a significant management science dimension. Deegan has recently completed the development of a conceptual model consisting of static elements (data model) and dynamic elements (transaction and state change specifications) as the basis for implementing management control systems in manufacturing. The results of this research are included in his Ph.D. thesis.

OR DEPARTMENT PROJECTS

The Department is actively involved in several contracted applied research projects with various commercial organisations within Ireland. One of these projects entitled *The Reduction of Milk Assembly Costs through On-Line Computer Control* was jointly financed by the IDA, NBST and Golden Vale Co-operative Creameries Ltd. This research project was carried out by the author. Also involved was Professor M L Fisher, Professor of Decision Sciences at the Wharton School, University of Pennsylvania.

The late Dr P F Perry was involved in an on-going project on *A Natural Resource Information System for Ireland* under Contract CP-133 between UCD and Directorate General 13 of the European Commission, together with Professor Frank Convery and John Blackwell of the Resource and Environmental Policy Centre at UCD. David McColl was the Project Director. The information system will consist of economic, techno-economic and relevant parameters describing the main characteristics of Irish natural resources including energy, minerals, forestry, demography, water resources, air resources and agriculture. Already a computerised system of forestry and demographic information has been implemented on the Amdahl 470/V8 computer system using the SPIRES (Stanford Public Information Retrieval System) database management system. This is currently accessed via a managed X.25 gateway to external national and international network-based information systems and users. It is intended to fully commercialise the system after the development phase at UCD to service from a single location inquiries for information on Irish natural resources from throughout the EEC and elsewhere.

Another of Dr Perry's research projects was the *Development of an Expert System for Lot Sizing.* This collaborative project with F Drechsler, of the Department of Industrial Management at Trinity College Dublin, and R Vail, now with the Centre for Management Studies at Oxford University, has been partially funded under the ESPRIT project. The expert system shell using ESP Advisor is linked to the Nixdorf COMET TOP manufacturing management information system and applies heuristic rules to identify and apply the lot-sizing algorithm most appropriate to the requirements of a given manager's situation.

SOME RECENT PUBLICATIONS

Harrison, H. C. Management science and productivity improvement in Irish milk co-operatives. *Interfaces,* Vol. 16, No. 4, July/August 1986, pp. 31-40.

Harrison, H. C. The electronic digital computer and *Melopsittacus undulatus. Interfaces,* Vol. 14, No. 4, July/August 1984, pp. 16-23.

Harrison, H. C. Restructuring for improved efficiency in the AgriBusiness sector of the Irish economy. In *Operational Research,* J. Brans (Ed). Elsevier Pubs. BV (North Holland),

1984, pp. 185-196.

Perry, P. F. Policy simulation in the natural resource sector. *Simulation,* September 1986.

Perry, P. F. Dual coordination for decomposed dynamic optimisation problems. *Journal of Civil Engineering Systems,* Vol. 3, March 1986, pp. 43-49.

Perry, P. F. Spatial and time decomposition algorithms for dynamic non-linear network optimisation using duality. *Journal of Optimisation Theory and Applications,* Vol. 42, No. 1, January 1984, pp. 77-101.

Deegan, A. J. and Timlin, J. C. Computer chargeback: The Irish experience. *Journal of Irish Business and Administrative Research,* Vol. 4, No. 1, April 1982, pp. 87-98.

Deegan, A. J. and Perry, P. F. Computer-integrated manufacturing: Research directions. *Journal of Irish Business and Administrative Research,* Vol. 5, No. 2, October 1983, pp. 27-40.

OR in University College Galway (UCG)

M E J O'KELLY

The first course in Operations Research at UCG was given in the late 1960s by the Department of Civil Engineering as a final year optional course for civil engineers. This course is still on offer and is concerned with the application of OR techniques to civil engineering problems.

With the establishment of UCG's Department of Industrial Engineering in 1971, courses in OR were offered to commerce and science students as well as to civil and industrial engineering students. In the early 1970s, the courses on offer were technique-oriented with an emphasis, particularly for engineering students, on understanding the mathematical foundations of these techniques. The orientation was applied OR and the course content reflected the background and professional interests of the students at both undergraduate and postgraduate level. The teaching approach used was to assist the students in using OR in their professional work. The idea was that 'operations research type thinking' would develop the critical faculties of the student, especially in the area of the use, and indeed abuse, of quantitative analysis.

From the mid-1970s onwards, the Department of Industrial Engineering began to offer, in addition to courses on techniques, courses of a more reflective or philosophical nature in OR. Considerable emphasis was devoted to problem-formulation, analysis of language and impact of political and societal environments on decision-making. Around the same time, separate courses in simulation and more advanced technique-oriented courses were offered. By the early 1980s, there was in place a set of courses covering the full range, from beginning undergraduate courses in OR techniques to postgraduate courses on the methodology of OR for students in commerce, engineering and science with a suitable mathematical background.

These are a few courses in which 'Operations Research' appears in the title. However, much of OR is taught in courses bearing titles such as management science, production analysis, production policy, computer-aided manufacturing, manufacturing engineering, analysis of manufacturing systems, quantitative analysis and quality and reliability engineering. This diversity of titles indicates the role played by OR in the formation of commerce, engineering and science students.

For industrial engineering degree students, it is not sufficient that they be aware of classical inventory modelling as normally understood by OR analysts. Their knowledge of materials management must go well beyond classical EOQ formulations, single and multi-period inventory probabilistic models. It must include an appreciation of approaches such as Materials Requirement Planning I (MRPI), Manufacturing Requirements Planning II (MRPII), Just in Time (JIT), Kanban and others not normally considered under the banner of OR. These students must realise that there is a materials system and that their knowledge of OR will assist in modelling the system. Similarly, they need to understand what is meant by a solution to the decision problems posed to the material manager and how such a solution can be evaluated. Furthermore, they should know that not all inventory problems can be solved using elegant algebraic manipulation and that simulation may be the way forward in practice.

In student project work, which is an essential element of all degree and diploma courses in industrial engineering, students are expected to bring their knowledge of OR to bear on the problem-formulation and solution stage of the project. Most of these projects are concerned with real decision-making problems in industry and services, and the student has the benefit of learning from an industry-based supervisor as well as from the academic supervisor. The project provides an ideal opportunity for students to understand, at first hand, the difficulties associated with decision problem-formulation and solution and the impact political and personality factors have in practice.

Over the past few years a few engineering students have

expressed a wish to pursue research degrees in 'pure' OR. Such students are being encouraged, but obtaining a reasonable level of financial support for them is a difficulty. In general, it seems that Irish industry is willing to support applied OR work in simulation, materials management or quality control, but is not yet ready to sponsor a graduate student interested, say, in investigating queueing theory in a fundamental way. In our experience, foreign students seem to be able to obtain fundings which allows them to work on more academic and less applied problems in OR. However, many students reading for a master's degree in industrial engineering write a research dissertation in the area of applied OR. The majority of these dissertations involve the building of simulation models of manufacturing systems, often modelling information flows, plant and equipment, and worker behaviour.

As far as commerce students are concerned, work in OR is considered part of their education in quantitative analysis and management information systems. The emphasis again tends to be on applied OR mainly in the operations and production management areas, with considerably less applications work in the other managerial functional areas. Only a few science students follow courses in OR in UCG, mainly perhaps because of the manner in which OR courses developed at Galway.

As there is no Department of Operations Research as such in UCG, formally there are no appointments in OR. However, about three or four members of the academic staff would probably consider that they are essentially operations researchers. Another three or four members of staff could certainly undertake an OR study, but would probably consider their main professional interests to be outside the immediate area of OR.

Interests of staff members in OR, broadly defined, include mathematical modelling of production systems, manpower analysis and modelling, reliability analysis, simulation, methodology of OR, quality assurance, mathematical statistical testing, ergonomic modelling and the use of artificial intelligence and heuristics in decision-support systems.

The area of industrial engineering is a prolific area for applied OR work. As the graduate school in industrial engineering develops, it is likely that more fundamental work in the area of OR will be undertaken in UCG.

OR in the University of Ulster (UU)

SALLY McCLEAN

In the early 1970s, an undergraduate course in Mathematics and Operational Research was introduced to the then New University of Ulster by Professor Andrew Young. This course comprised a core of mainstream mathematics units, supplemented by economics, accountancy and computing science units in the first two years of the degree. In the final year, three units of OR were studied – covering linear and dynamic programming, game theory, sequencing, replacement models, stock control, queues, stochastic processes, simulation, optimisation and forecasting. These units were supplemented by three additional units from statistics, numerical analysis or economics.

The Mathematics and Operational Research degree has attracted a steady, if small, stream of students who are less interested in the more rigorous aspects of mathematics and more inclined towards applying their subject to the 'real world'. These graduates have found employment in a variety of posts in education, business and government.

In 1982, a new undergraduate course in Statistics, Computing and Operational Research was introduced. This degree replaces more rigorous mathematics with a larger component of computing science in response to the increasing demand for graduates skilled in computer techniques and able to apply these techniques to the practice of OR.

However, it is at the postgraduate level that NUU (now the University of Ulster) has made most impact on the teaching of OR in Ireland. A number of Ph.D. theses have been concerned with manpower planning – developing models for a number of Irish, UK and international firms. More recently, one Ph.D. has been completed on nurse manpower planning and several are nearing completion. Other successful Ph.D. topics have been modelling the life cycle of liver fluke, in conjunction with Trinity College and An Foras Talúntais; modelling the British and Greek education systems; a manpower analysis of telephone expansion; and techniques for assessing nurse training and education. Ph.D. students are currently working on nurse manpower analysis, inventory models and optimisation of databases. The Ph.D. graduates are now in a variety of educational and business establishments throughout the world and continue to apply operational research techniques to the problems of their own countries (*below*).

The development and success of OR at NUU has been entirely due to Professor Andrew Young whose keen interest in the subject, and desire to apply mathematics to practical problems, has led to the successful application of OR to so many substantive areas. Along with his staff and research students he has, since its inception, been a keen and energetic member of ORMSI and, until his retirement in 1983, never missed an annual conference. The author now teaches all OR courses in Coleraine; Norman Smith teaches OR at Jordanstown.

PH.D. GRADUATE EMPLOYMENT

George Gettinby: Senior Lecturer in Mathematics, University of Strathclyde.

Panos Vassiliou: Professor of Statistics, University of Thessalonika, Greece.

George Agrafiotis: Lecturer in Statistics, University of Athens.

Sally McClean: Lecturer in Mathematics, University of Ulster.

Tunji Abodunde: OPEC Secretariat, Vienna.

Demetrios Karageorgos: Ministry of Education, Greece.

Akinrimlola Falodi: Lecturer in Mathematics, Nigeria.

Norma Reid: Director of the Centre for Applied Health Studies and Senior Lecturer in Mathematics, University of Ulster.

PH.D. THESES

George Gettinby (1974) *Mathematical Models for the Control of Liver Fluke Infection.*

Various models for the life cycle and control of liver fluke infection in sheep are described. The models are used to establish and measure the success of the control techniques developed.

Panos Vassiliou (1974) *Mathematical models in manpower systems.*

Various non-linear models are developed which relate promotions to vacancies, as well as numbers available for promotion, and take into account the expectations of staff. Wastage rates are related to a concept of cumulative acceleration of the overall growth of the firm.

George Agrafiotis (1975) *Stochastic models for manpower planning.*

A network model is developed to model the movements of staff through the various grades. The manpower system is also described as a semi-Markov process which allows various distributions to be used for length of stay in a grade.

Sally McClean (1975) *Stochastic models for manpower systems for several British and Irish firms.*

Data from eight firms was used to test well-established models such as the lognormal and transition. Stochastic models of staff flows through the system were then developed. Finally a model of manpower growth was produced which related growth in staff size to that of capital.

Tunji Abodunde (1977) *Recruitment control for manpower planning.*

The linear programming approach is used to provide a means of controlling the number of people in each grade of an organisation. This enables a schedule of recruitment to be developed.

Demetrios Karageorgos (1977) *Mathematical models in educational planning.*

Models are developed to predict the numbers of pupils and teachers in primary and secondary education. These models were tested using data from both Northern Ireland and Greece and shown to give a good fit over several years.

Joseph Akinbade (1978) *Operational Research applications to Nigerian small and medium size industries.*

A structuring approach is used to identify the OR type problems that are most commonly experienced by small and medium size Nigerian firms. A taxonomic classification of problem types and industry classes is carried out and the OR methods used by various firms are surveyed.

Akinrimlola Falodi (1978) *A model to determine the producer prices of Nigerian agricultural export crops.*

The past performance of Nigerian agricultural boards is reviewed and new pricing policies formulated that will provide an incentive to increase production. These policies are then compared with existing ones.

Norma Reid (1983) *A multivariate statistical investigation of the factors affecting nurse training in the clinical area.*

The criteria which determine the suitability of a clinical area for nurse training are examined and the number of learners who can be effectively supported is determined.

Hilary McCartney (1986) *Nurse manpower planning in Northern Ireland.*

Manpower models were developed to describe the patterns of wastage, service and promotion for Northern Ireland nurses. These models were tested on DHSS data, consisting of information on each nurse in Northern Ireland in employment in the Health Service since 1977.

RESEARCH PAPERS

Young, A. Demographic and ecological models for manpower planning. In *Aspects of Manpower Planning* (Eds. D. J. Bartholomew and B. R. Morris), The English Universities Press Ltd, 1971.

The lognormal and transition models for wastage are fitted to data from a large international firm. A non-linear model of promotion is developed which combines an ecological principle for numbers promoted with a 'frustration factor' for staff who leave having been overlooked for promotion.

Gettinby, G. Assessment of the effectiveness of control techniques for liver fluke infection. In *Ecological Stability* (Eds. M. B. Usher and M. W. Williamson), Chapman and Hall Ltd, 1973.

Simulation of the statistical models establishes quantitative relationships that enable the success of control techniques for liver fluke to be measured.

Young, A. and Vassiliou, P-C. G. A non-linear model of the promotion of staff. *JRSS,* No. A137, 1974, pp. 584-593.
Non-linear models of manpower planning are developed which relate promotions to vacancies, as well as numbers available for promotion. These models are compared with the linear transition model.

Gettinby, G., Grainger, J. N. R., and Hope-Cawdery, M. J. Forecasting the incidence of Fascioliases from climatic data. *Int. J. Biom.,* No. 18, 1974, pp. 319-323.
A fluke-forecasting system is produced based on the mortality and development rates within the lifecycle in relation to temperature. This provides some information on animal infectivity patterns and how they vary from year to year and with geographical location.

Vassiliou, P-C. G. A Markov chain model for the prediction of wastage in a manpower system. *Operat. Res. Quart.* No. 27, 1976, pp. 57-70.
Wastage rates are related to a concept of cumulative acceleration of the overall growth of the firm. This is developed in the context of a Markov chain model.

McClean, S. I. The two stage model of personnel behaviour. *JRSS,* No. A139, 1976, pp. 205-217.
A two-stage continuous time Markov model is developed where recruits enter a first stage of being 'uncommitted', which has a high leaving rate, before entering a second 'committed' stage, with a lower leaving rate. The model was tested on 8 firms.

McClean, S. I. Some models for company growth. *JRSS,* No. A139, 1976, pp. 501-507.
A stochastic model is developed which describes the growth of a firm by considering the number of employees and its capital resources as interacting processes. The model was fitted to 6 firms from the 'Times 1000'.

Young, A. and Abodunde, T. Personnel recruitment policies and long-term production planning. *Journal of the Operational Research Society,* No. 30, 1978, pp. 225-236.
A schedule of recruitment is developed for expansion in the workforce to develop the telephone network in the Republic of Ireland. Linear programming is used as a means of controlling the number of people in each grade.

McClean, S. I. and Abodunde, T. Entropy as a measure of stability in a manpower system. *Journal of the Operational Research Society,* No. 29, 1978, pp. 885-889.
Shannon entropy is used as a measure of the stability of the length of service distribution of a firm. This is applied both to the present structure of a firm to enable day-to-day comparisons to be made and to the steady state distribution which allows inter-firm comparisons.

Gettinby, G. and McClean S. I. A matrix formulation of the life-cycle of liver fluke. *Proc. of the Royal Irish Academy.* Vol. 79B, 1979, pp. 155-167.
A matrix model of the life-cycle is developed which takes into account the various biological stages of parasite development and also climatic

features which make the transition matrix time-dependent. The model is used to test the effectiveness of various control strategies.

McClean, S. I. and Karageorgos, D. L. An age-stratified manpower model applied to the education system. *The Statistician,* No. 28, 1979, pp. 9-18.

A transition model is developed which uses as classes the number of teachers in each age group. The steady state distribution is discussed and some statistical results presented. This theory is then applied to data for the Northern Ireland educational system.

Abodunde, T. T. and McClean, S. I. Production planning for a manpower system with a constant level of recruitment. 1980.

A continuous-time Markov model is developed which relates the number of staff in each grade of the workforce to the number of telephones installed in the Republic of Ireland. Expressions are given for the means and variances at any time for the number in each grade and also the number of telephones in the system.

Young, A. *Factors affecting recruitment and wastage of nurses in Northern Ireland.* Report to DHSS (Northern Ireland), 1982.

This report describes the patterns of wastage, service and promotion, including part-time and broken service, and patterns of rejoining service for all the nurses employed by the Health Service in Northern Ireland between 1977 and 1982. Patterns of recruitment are also discussed and manpower models developed.

Reid, N. G. *Wards in Chancery? Nurse training in the clinical area.* Royal College of Nursing research series, 1985.

The criteria which determine the suitability of a clinical area for nurse training are examined in this book. The number of leavers who can be effectively supported is then estimated.

Reid, N. G. The effective training of nurses: Manpower implication. *Int. J. Nurs. Stud.,* No. 22, 1985, pp. 89-98.

Estimates of times required for training which were provided by 'Wards in Chancery?' *(above)* for hospital and college-based staff are used to calculate the manpower implication of an effective system of nurse education.

McClean, S. I. Estimation for the mixed exponential distribution using grouped follow-up data. *Applied Statistics,* No. 35, 1986, pp. 31-37.

The mixed exponential distribution is fitted to 3 grades of nurses from the Northern Ireland Health Service and shown to give a good fit to leaving distributions.

McClean, S. I. Extending the entropy stability measure for manpower systems. *J. Operational Research Soc. (to appear).*

The continuous version of the Shannon entropy function is used as a stability measure for length of service distributions. This is similar to the demographic entropy measure for a population. The measure is applied to data from the Northern Ireland nursing service.

Reid, N. G. Recent manpower trends in Northern Ireland. *Int. J. Nurs. Stud.,* No. 23, 1986, pp. 199-210.

Trends in leaving, recruitment and movements in and out of 'limbo' are discussed for the Northern Ireland nursing service from 1978-84. The analysis is also broken down by age for different grades of nurses.

Reid, N. G. Nurse manpower: The problems ahead. *Int. J. Nurs. Stud.* No. 23, 1986, pp. 186-197.

Forecasting manpower needs for the UK is discussed in terms of demand, wastage in training, qualified wastage and the mix of entrants and re-entrants. It is concluded that the transfer of nurse training into higher education would help considerably in solving the manpower crisis.

CHAPTER NOTES AND REFERENCES

CHAPTER 2
1. O'Donovan, T. *VisiCalc made simple*. Wiley, Chichester and New York, 1984.

CHAPTER 3
1. Rivett, P. and Ackoff, R. L. *A Manager's Guide to Operational Research*. Wiley, Chichester and New York, 1963.
2. Shycon, H. N. Perspectives on MS Application. *Interfaces*, Vol. 2, No. 4, 1972.

CHAPTER 5
1. Foley, M. A. Operations Research in Aer Lingus. *Journal of the Royal Aeronautical Society*, Vol. 72-691, July 1968.
2. Davidson, J. D. Four Vice-Presidents, Three Directors, and a Partridge in a Pear Tree. *Proceedings of 20th AGIFORS Symposium*, 1980.
3. Foley, M. A. Inventory Control in Aer Lingus. *Proceedings of 5th AGIFROS Symposium*, 1965.
4. Wagner, H. *Principles of Operations Research*. Prentice Hall, Englewood Cliffs, New Jersey, 1969.
5. Mitchell, G. Problems of controlling slow-moving spares. *OR Quarterly*, Vol. 13, No. 1, 1962.
6. Flinter, M. Internal Aer Lingus Report, 1976.
7. Sweeney, B. Development of Material Management in SCEPTRE. *Proceedings of 23rd AGIFORS Symposium*, 1983.
8. Johnston, R. H. W. and McNamara, P. Long-term Route Profitability and the spreading of Overhead Costs. *Proceedings of 9th AGIFORS Symposium*, 1969.
9. Johnston, R. H. W. and O'Siochru, O. Long-term Fleet Planning as a step towards an Integral Company Model. *Proceedings of 5th AGIFORS Symposium*, 1965.
10. Johnston, R. H. W. A Computerised Capacity Planning System. *Proceedings of 8th AGIFORS Symposium*, 1968.
11. Kennedy, D. Internal Aer Lingus Report, 1963.
12. Walsh, P. D. K. Internal Aer Lingus Report, 1973.
13. O'Broin, S. P. Manpower Planning for Airport Operations. *Proceedings of 8th AGIFORS Symposium*, 1968.
14. Foley, M. A., Flinter, M. and Lynch, J. M. Internal Aer Lingus Report, 1967.
15. Lennon, C. O. Long-range Evaluation of Hangar Capacity. *Proceedings of 11th AGIFORS Symposium*, 1971.
16. Foley, D. Internal Aer Lingus Report, 1986.

17. Saaty, T. L. *Elements of Queueing Theory*. McGraw-Hill, 1961.
18. Johnston, R. H. W. An Analytical Approach to the Simulation of a Real-time System. *Proceedings of 5th AGIFORS Symposium*, 1965.
19. MacAirt, J. G. Financial Advantages of eliminating Error No-shows in a Reservations System. *Proceedings of 7th AGIFORS Symposium*, 1967.
20. O'Broin, S. P. and Flinter, M. Internal Aer Lingus Report, 1969.
21. Napoli, J. G. Determining Station Stockout Rates for Rotable Spare Parts in an Airline System. *Proceedings of 1st AGIFORS Symposium*, 1961.

CHAPTER 6

1. Divilly, P., O'Hogan, D. and Rodgers, M. *An evaluation by simulation of the profitability of the production of flax in Ireland*. Statistics Department, TCD, 1971 (unpublished).
2. The 'retting' process involves the preferential degradation of the cellulose, leaving the fibre intact. This used to be done anaerobically in ponds, giving a characteristic offensive odour (the 'wet-retting' process). 'Dew retting' takes place if flax is simply left to lie in the field after pulling, to be attacked by soil bacteria under moist conditions.
3. Carroll B., Conlon, T. and Herlihy, P. *A study of milk collection and quality control at Lough Egish*. Statistics Department, TCD, 1973 (unpublished).
4. Howlett, N., Logan, J. and O'Brien, D. *The effects of the supply pattern of milk on the dairy processing industry*. Statistics Department, TCD, 1972 (unpublished).
5. Hooper, L., Lyons, D. and Murphy, M. *The relationship between seasonality and profitability on Irish dairy farms*. Statistics Department, TCD, 1972 (unpublished).
6. Ní Eigeartaigh, A. and Franklin, G. *A deterministic simulation of locomotive allocation in the Irish rail system*. Statistics Department, TCD, 1971 (unpublished).
7. Redmond, A., Roden, J. and McQuillan, D. *A computer model of a school*. Statistics Department, TCD, 1973 (unpublished).
8. Hickey, J., Kinsella, I. and O'Kane, C. *A preliminary approach to computer model building in horticulture*. Statistics Department, TCD, 1971 (unpublished).
9. Neenan, M. and Devereux, J. Some recent researches on the growing of fibre flax. *Procs. R.I.A.*, 1973.
10. In 1986, a new procedure was developed in which the flax is pulled, transported and stored centrally for retting under controlled conditions, using a bacterial culture spray. This process, which avoids the uncertainties of autumnal weather, deserves to succeed.
11. These are generic names for classes of bacteria, defined by their preferred temperature range.
12. This concept has tranferred itself from quantum mechanics, where Heisenberg discovered that if you observe a phenomenon, by the very act of observing it you interfere with it; the famous 'uncertainty prin-

ciple' follows. In the present context, the author is talking about a macroscopic analogue.

13. du Vivier, R. *Agriculture and the environment.* European Parliament, A2207/85, February 1986.

This report produces evidence, mostly from France and Germany, that the switch from intensive, industrial-style monocrop production back towards more traditional agriculture practice, with scientific support from biology (primarily ecology) rather than chemistry, while producing less output per hectare would require substantially less bought-in inputs. The net earnings per farm would be improved and the earning per worker of the expanded workforce would be unchanged. Long-term conservation of the soil is possible only with biological agriculture; under intensive practices, the soil is reduced to the status of a devitalised mechanical substrate for chemically fed crops and tends to degrade towards dust or clay. It takes 2 to 3 years to revitalise soil under a biological regime: earthworm power replaces tractor power (ie biological soils require less mechanical effort to produce a good tilth).

The du Vivier Report constitutes a time-bomb under the EEC's Common Agricultural Policy (CAP). It is, of course, being vehemently opposed by the agrichemical interests and to date has largely been ignored by the agricultural research establishment.

14. The author is indebted to Alan Matthews and Julian MacAirt for drawing his attention to the following relevant works:

Riemsdijk, J. van. A system of direct compensation payments to farmers. *European Review of Agricultural Economics.* Vol. 1, No. 2, 1973, pp. 161-189.

Tarditi, S. Price policies and European integration. In *Price and market policies in European agriculture,* K. Thomsen and R. Warren (Eds). University of Newcastle-upon-Tyne, 1984.

Koeke, U. and Tangermann, S. Supplementing farm price policy by direct income payments. *European Review of Agricultural Economics,* Vol. 4, No. 1, 1977, pp. 7-31.

Castle, B., Woltjer, E. and Pisani, E. (Socialist group of the European Parliament). *Reform of the Common Agricultural Policy.* Document COM (86) 199 of 23/5/86 of the EEC Commission.

This paper discusses the impact of the Socialists' proposals on the idea of paying farmers for environmental management.

CHAPTER 7

1. Booth, J. L. *Fuel and Power in Ireland.* Parts I-III (1966) and Part IV (1967). Economic and Social Research Institute, Dublin.

2. *Report by the ESB Investigation Committee (The Fletcher Report).* Stationery Office, Dublin, 1970.

3. Bunyan, R. J. *Ireland and Natural Gas.* United Dominion Trust (Ireland) Ltd., Dublin, 1974.

4. Operations Research Section, Department of the Public Service. *Ireland's Energy Usage and Requirements – Interim Report.* Dublin, 1975.

5. Henry, E. *Energy Conservation in Ireland 1975-1985*. Report to the Minister for Transport and Power, Stationery Office, Dublin, 1976.

6. Department of Industry, Commerce and Energy. *Energy-Ireland: Discussion Document on Some Current Energy Problems and Options*. Stationery Office, Dublin, July 1978.

7. Geraghty, D. *Reference Energy Systems 1974, 1985 and 2000*. National Science Council, Dublin, 1977.

8. Brady, J. and Kavanagh, R. *Energy Supply and Demand – The Next 30 Years*. National Board for Science and Technology, Dublin, 1980.

9. Abilock, H. and Fishbone, L. *Users' guide for Markal, IEA Systems Analysis Project*. Brookhaven National Laboratory, New York, 1979.

10. Abilock, H. and Fishbone, L. Markal: A Linear Programming Model for Energy Systems Analysis. Technical Description of the Brookhaven National Laboratory Version. *Energy Research*, Vol. 5, 1981, pp. 353-375.

11. Brady, J. *Energy Technology after the '80s*. National Board for Science and Technology, Dublin, 1983.

12. Kavanagh, R. and Killen, L. *Energy Forecasts for Ireland*. National Board for Science and Technology, Dublin, 1980.

13. Kavanagh, R. and Killen, L. Energy Demand Projections and Preliminary Assessment of Conservation Potential. *Irish Journal of Environmental Science*, Vol. 1, No. 2, 1981.

14. Killen, L. *Energy Forecasts for Ireland*. National Board for Science and Technology, Dublin, 1981.

15. Henry, E. *Demand for Electricity up to 1990: A Forecasting Model with Numerical Results*. Economic and Social Research Institute, Dublin, 1979.

16. Brady, J., Henry, E. and Kavanagh, R. Reconciliation of the Results of an Energy Optimisation Model with a General Economic Profile. Procs. *International Conference on Energy Systems Analysis*, Dublin, October 1979.

17. Scott, S. *Energy Demand in Ireland, Projections and Policy*. Economic and Social Research Institute, Dublin, 1980.

18. Kavanagh, R. and Killen, L. *Energy Flow Optimisation Model-Ireland. Final Report to the Commission of the European Communities*. National Board for Science and Technology, Dublin, 1980.

19. Guilmot, J.-F., McGlue, D., Valette, P. and Waeterloos, C. *Energie 2000 – Une Projection de reference et ses Variantes pour la Communaute Europeene et la Monde a l'Horizon 2000*. Commission des Communautes Europeenes, Economica, Paris, 1986.

20. Kavanagh, R., Coffey, P. and Murphy, C. *Towards a Model of the Milled Peat Production System. Peat and the Environment, 1985*. International Peat Society Symposium, Jonkoping, Sweden, 17-20 September 1985.

CHAPTER 8

1. Gordon, G. *Systems Simulation*. Prentice Hall, Englewood Cliffs, New Jersey, 1978.

2. Neelamkavil, F. *Computer Simulation and Modelling*. John Wiley and Sons, London, 1986.

3. 'Student'. The probable error of a mean. *Biometrika*, Vol. 6, No. 1, 1908, pp. 1-25.
4. Lehmer, D. H. Mathematical methods in large-scale computing units. *Annals Computer Lab.*, Harvard University, Vol. 26, 1951, pp. 141-146.
5. Kleijnen, J. P. C. Selecting random number seeds in practice. *Simulation*, Vol. 47, No. 1, 1986, pp. 15-19.
6. Knuth, D. E., *The Art of Computer Programming, Vol. 2.* Addison Wesley, London, 1969.
7. Society for Computer Simulation (SCS). Catalogue of Simulation Software. *Simulation*, Vol. 45, No. 4, 1985, pp. 196-209.
8. O'Donovan, T. *GPSS: Simulation made simple.* John Wiley and Sons, London, 1979.
9. Bobillier, P. A., Kahan, B. C. and Probst, A. R. *Simulation with GPSS and GPSS V.* Prentice Hall, Englewood Cliffs, New Jersey, 1976.
10. Kleijnen, J. P. C. *Statistical techniques in Simulation, Part 1 & 2.* Marcel Dekker, New York, 1974-75.
11. IBM. *System/360 Continuous System Modelling Program. User's Manual and CSMP III Manual.* IBM Corp., White Plains, New York, 1972.
12. Francis, N. D. *Computable Models in National Educational Planning.* Research Report, Dept. of Computer Science, TCD, 1971.
13. Francis, N. D. Simulation of Operating Systems – a functional flow chart. *ACM Operating Systems Review*, Vol. 19, No. 3, 1980, pp. 16-21.
14. Francis, N. D. and Neelamkavil, J. D. Computer-aided production planning in a tyre factory. *Economic Computation and Econ. Cybernetics Studies and Research*, Vol. 14, No. 3, 1980, pp. 91-103.
15. Francis, N. D. Simulation of a manufacturing system. In *Proceedings of 1981 UKSC Conference on Computer Simulation.* IPC Science and Technology Press, 1981, pp. 90-96.
16. Francis, N. D. and Fleming, D. I. Optimum allocation of places to students in a national university system. *BIT*, Vol. 25, No. 2, 1985, pp. 307-317.
17. Ryan, K. T. *The development and evaluation of simulation models for bus operations planning.* Ph.D. thesis, TCD, 1977.
18. Ryan, K. T. Validating a bus operations simulation model. In *Proceedings IEEE, Winter Simulation Conference.* 1979, pp. 483-495.
19. Hayes-Roth, F., Waterman, D. A. and Lenat, D. B. *Building expert systems.* Addison Wesley, Reading, Mass., 1983.
20. O'Keefe, R. M. Simulation and expert systems – A taxonomy and some examples. *Simulation*, Vol. 46, No. 1, 1986, pp. 10-16.
21. Klahr, P. AI approaches to Simulation. In *Proc. UKSC Conf. on Comp. Simulation*, 1984, pp. 87-92.
22. Nance, R. E. and Overstreet, C. M. A specification language to assist in analysis of discrete event simulation models. *CACM*, Vol. 28, No. 2, 1985, pp. 190-201.
23. Oren, T. J. Concepts and criteria to assess acceptability of simulation studies: A frame reference. *CACM*, Vol. 24, No. 4, 1981, pp. 180-189.

CHAPTER 9
1. Sandilands, F. (Chairman). *Inflation account up: Report of Inflation Accounting Committee.* HMSO, 1975.

ABBREVIATIONS

The following abbreviations are used throughout the text of this book:

AFT	An Foras Talúntais (Agricultural Institute)
AGIFORS	Airline Group International Federation of Operations Research Societies
AI	Artificial Intelligence
AIB	Allied Irish Banks
ALT	Aer Lingus Teoranta (Irish Airline)
B of I	Bank of Ireland
CAO	Central Applications Office
CCA	Current Cost Accounting
CEO	Chief Executive Officer
CIE	Córas Iompair Éireann (Irish transport company)
CPI	Consumer Price Index
CPP	Current Purchasing Power
DBA	Diploma in Business Administration
DHSS	Department of Health and Social Security
DPS	Department of Public Service
DSS	Decision Support System
EHSSB	Eastern Health and Social Services Board
EJOR	European Journal of Operations Research
EOQ	Economic Order Quantity
ERI	Economic Research Institute
ESB	Electricity Supply Board
ESRI	Economic and Social Research Institute
FIFO	First in First out
GLC	Greater London Council
GNP	Gross National Product
HCA	Historic Cost Accounting
IBAR	Irish Business and Administrative Research
IDA	Industrial Development Authority
IFORS	International Federation of Operations Research Societies
IIRS	Institute for Industrial Research and Standards
IMI	Irish Management Institute
IPA	Institute of Public Administration
ISBN	International Standard Book Number
JRSS	Journal of Royal Statistical Society
JFK	John F Kennedy airport
LP	Linear Programming
MBA	Master of Business Administration

MIS	Management Information Systems
MS	Management Science
MSISS	Management Science and Industrial Systems Studies
NBST	National Board for Science and Technology
NCEA	National Council for Educational Awards
NET	Nítrigin Éireann Teoranta (Irish fertiliser company)
NIHE	National Institute for Higher Education, Limerick
NIHED	National Institute for Higher Education, Dublin
NUU	New University of Ulster
ORMSI	Operations Research and Management Science Society of Ireland
ORSI	Operations Research Society of Ireland (former name of ORMSI)
P & T	Post and Telegraphs, Department of
PBT	Profit before Tax
PERT	Program Evaluation and Review Technique
PR	Proportional Representation
QUB	Queen's University Belfast
R & D	Research and Development
RIA	Royal Irish Academy
ROL	Reorder Level
ROQ	Reorder Quantity
RTC	Regional Technical College
RTE	Radio Telefís Éireann (Irish TV/Radio station)
SKC	Stokes Kennedy Crowley
TCD	Trinity College Dublin
UCC	University College Cork
UCD	University College Dublin
UCG	University College Galway
UU	University of Ulster
VLSI	Very Large Scale Integration

SUBJECT INDEX

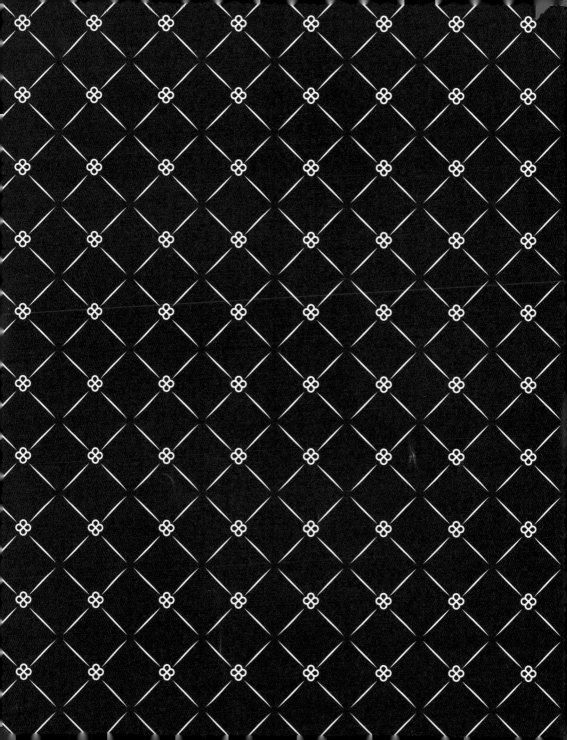

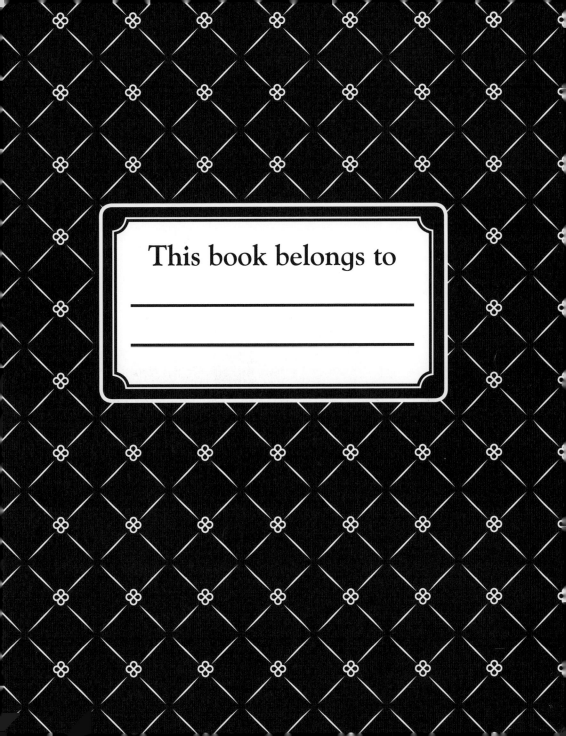

This book belongs to

This edition published by Parragon Books Ltd in 2015

Parragon Books Ltd
Chartist House
15–17 Trim Street
Bath BA1 1HA, UK
www.parragon.com

ISBN 978-1-4748-0641-1

Printed in China

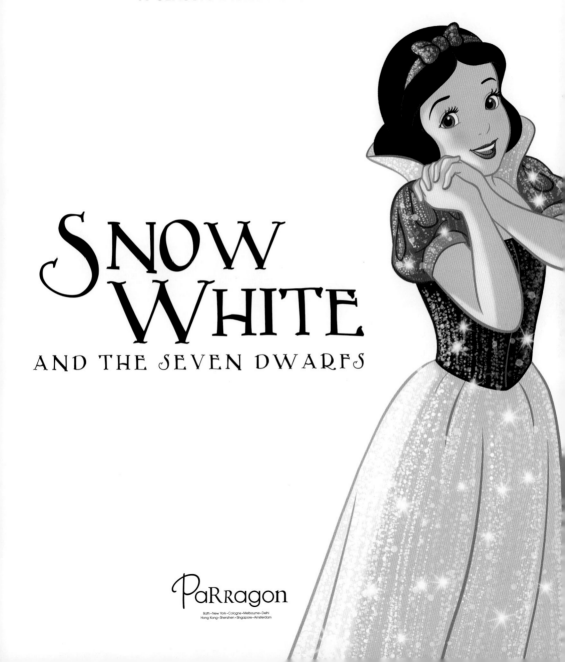

DISNEY MOVIE COLLECTION
A CLASSIC DISNEY STORYBOOK SERIES

SNOW WHITE
AND THE SEVEN DWARFS

PaRRagon

Bath • New York • Cologne • Melbourne • Delhi
Hong Kong • Shenzhen • Singapore • Amsterdam

Once upon a time, there lived a beautiful princess named Snow White. Her stepmother, the Queen, was jealous of Snow White's beauty.

Every day the Queen asked her mirror, "Magic
Mirror on the wall, who is the fairest one of all?"
Each time the mirror would answer, "You are."
But one day the mirror replied, "A lovely maid
I see, who is more fair than thee."
"It's Snow White!" snarled the Queen.

Snow White was in the courtyard, singing as she went about her chores.

A handsome young prince was riding by and heard her lovely voice. He climbed the castle wall to find her but Snow White was shy and ran up to her balcony.

From the courtyard below, the Prince sang
to Snow White and she listened happily.

She placed a kiss on a friendly dove, who
carried it to the Prince below.

At that very moment, the jealous Queen was plotting against Snow White. She ordered her royal huntsman to take Snow White far into the forest and kill her.

Afraid of angering the Queen, the huntsman took
Snow White into the forest to gather wild flowers.

Snow White kneeled to soothe a baby bird that had
fallen from its nest. "Oh, please don't cry," she said.

As she spoke, the huntsman crept up behind her
with his dagger at the ready.

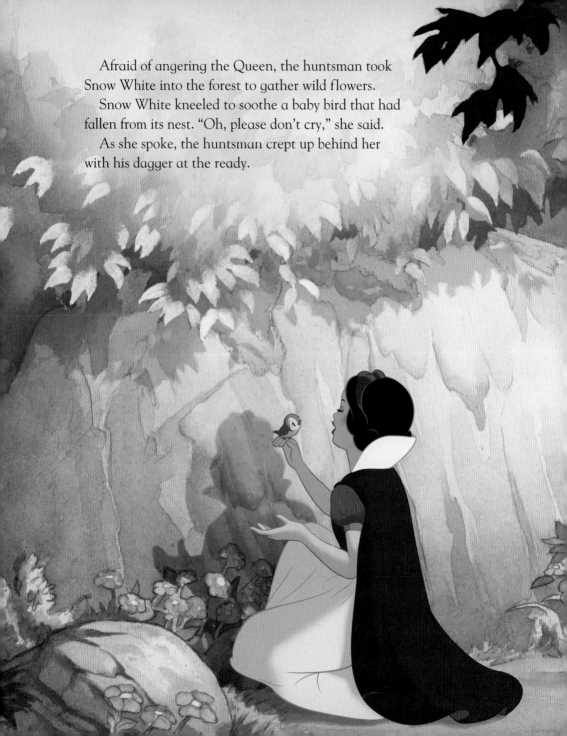

But the huntsman could not harm the gentle girl.
"Forgive me," he begged. Then he warned Snow White about
the Queen's evil plan. "Run away, child, and never come back!"

Snow White fled into the forest. As she ran, she felt eyes watching her. The trees seemed to reach out to grab her.

With nowhere left to run, she fell to the ground and began to cry.

After a while, Snow White looked up and found herself surrounded by forest animals. "Do you know where I can stay?" she asked them.

The friendly animals led Snow White to a tiny cottage
in the woods.

"It's like a doll's house!" said Snow White. She knocked
at the door but no one answered. "Please may I come in?"
she called. Still, there was no reply.

Slowly she stepped inside.

As Snow White wandered through the house, she discovered seven little chairs and seven little beds.

"Seven little children must live here! Let's clean the house and surprise them," the princess suggested. "Then maybe they'll let me stay."

Close by, the seven dwarfs who owned the cottage were busy
working in their mine. All day long they dug for diamonds.

At five o'clock it was time to go. Doc led Grumpy, Happy,
Sleepy, Sneezy, Bashful and Dopey home, singing and whistling
as they went.

When the dwarfs reached their cottage the light was on – someone was in their house! They crept inside and tiptoed upstairs to find someone fast asleep beneath their blankets.

"It's a monster!" whispered one dwarf.

Stepping closer, Doc cried out, "Why, it's a girl!"
The dwarfs gazed at Snow White.
    "She's beautiful," Bashful said. "Just like an angel."

Snow White sat up and said, "How do you do?"
She explained to the dwarfs who she was and
what the evil Queen had planned for her.
"Don't send me away," she begged.

"If you let me stay, I'll wash and sew and sweep and cook,"
Snow White promised.

At that the dwarfs shouted, "Hooray! She stays!" And the
happy princess ran to the kitchen to prepare dinner.

The dwarfs rushed downstairs to eat, but Snow White
said, "Supper is not quite ready. You'll just have time to wash.
Let me see your hands."

They reluctantly showed their dirty hands to Snow White.
"Worse than I thought," she said. "March straight outside and
wash, or you won't get a bite to eat."

All the dwarfs but one headed to the tub.
"I'd like to see anybody make me wash!"
said Grumpy.

Just as Grumpy spoke, the other dwarfs
pounced on him and dumped him into the
tub. They scrubbed him squeaky-clean.

"You'll pay for this!" growled Grumpy.

Back at the castle, the Queen stood before her
Magic Mirror. "Who is the fairest of them all?" she
asked, as usual. But instead of answering as she had
expected, the mirror told her that Snow White was the
fairest in the land. She was still alive – the huntsman
had lied to her!

The mirror also told the Queen exactly where
Snow White was hiding.

The angry Queen drank a potion that disguised
her as an old hag. Then she created a magic apple.

"With one bite of this poisoned apple, Snow
White's eyes will close forever," she cackled. "Only a
kiss from her true love will wake her!"

Back at the cottage, Snow White and the
seven dwarfs were unaware of the Queen's
plot. They finished Snow White's delicious
dinner and then they sang and danced late
into the night.

Even Grumpy joined the fun, thumping
away on a pipe organ.

The next morning, Snow White kissed each dwarf goodbye
as he marched off to the mine. Dopey even managed to get
two kisses!

Doc warned the princess, "The Queen is a sly one. Beware
of strangers!"

"Don't let nobody or nothing in the house!" Grumpy added.

The Queen, disguised as the old hag, spent the whole night walking through the forest to the dwarfs' little home.

She waited in the shadows and watched the dwarfs leave. Then, slowly, she crept up to the cottage.

Snow White was busy making a pie when a shadow fell
over her. She looked up with a gasp and saw the old lady
at the window.

"All alone, my pet?" the Queen asked Snow White.
Then she offered the princess the poisoned apple.

"Go on, have a bite."

Snow White's bird friends knew the old woman was not
who she claimed to be. Before Snow White could take the
apple, the birds dived at the Queen, pecking her hair and
flapping their wings in her face, trying to drive her away.

"Shame on you, frightening an old lady," Snow White
scolded the birds. She felt sorry for the old woman and
helped her inside the cottage.

The birds and forest animals raced to the diamond mine to warn the dwarfs. They tugged on the dwarfs' beards and hats. They pulled their sleeves and pushed them from behind. At last, the dwarfs understood.

"The Queen! Snow White!" Doc cried.

"We've got to save her!" Grumpy shouted.

But before the dwarfs could get back to the cottage, Snow White took the poisoned fruit from the old lady and took a single bite.

Snow White fell to the ground, dropping the rest of the apple. "Now I'll be the fairest in the land!" cackled the Queen, as a huge thunderstorm began outside.

The Queen ran from the cottage and out into the rain. But before she could escape, the seven dwarfs and all the forest animals came charging at her through the trees.

"There she goes," cried Grumpy. "After her!"

Thunder boomed overhead and lightning struck all around, but the dwarfs kept on chasing the Queen. They climbed after her and cornered her at the top of a rocky cliff.

"I'll fix you!" she shrieked as she tried to roll an enormous boulder down on top of them.

Suddenly, a bolt of lighting struck the ledge where the Queen stood!

The rock crumbled beneath her feet and the evil Queen fell from the cliff and into the darkness below.

The heartbroken dwarfs built a beautiful bed for the sleeping Snow White and watched over her day and night. Then one day the Prince appeared in the forest clearing.

The handsome Prince had
searched far and wide for the girl
he had met at the well that
morning. When he came to the
clearing where Snow White lay,
he kneeled down and, with great
sorrow, kissed her farewell.
It was Love's First Kiss!

With a soft sigh, Snow White sat up and rubbed her eyes. The Prince shouted with joy and lifted her in his arms. The dwarfs danced and laughed and the woods rang with calls from the happy forest animals. Snow White was alive!

Snow White thanked the dwarfs for all they had done, then kissed each one goodbye, promising to see them again soon. Together, the Prince and Snow White rode off to his castle, where they lived happily ever after.